THROW AWAY THE CRUTCHES

Buildings Blocks to Unlocking
Your Personal Potential

James G. Floor

WITH CRAIG FERGUSON

Synergy
Publishing Group

Published by Synergy Publishing, a division of Synergy Communications Group.

Interior design and typography by Becky Earls.

Jacket design by Richmond and Williams, Inc.

Most Scripture quotations, unless otherwise indicated, are taken from *The Living Bible*. Used by permission, Tyndale House Publishers. Other Scripture quotations from the *New International Version©*. Copyright 1973, 1978, 1984 by International Bible Society. Used by permission of Zondervan Publishing House. All rights reserved.

"I Am A Promise" by William J. and Gloria Gaither, ©1975 by William J. Gaither. Used by permission.

ISBN 0-9655335-0-6

Printed in the United States of America

9 8 7 6 5 4 3 2 1 00 99 98 97

To my beautiful wife, Margee,
for her steadfast love and commitment;
to my lovely daughter, Megan,
for her strength and independence;
and to my talented son, Andrew,
for his humor and wit.

CONTENTS

"The ideas I stand for are not mine.
I borrowed them from Socrates. I swiped them from Chesterfield.
I stole them from Jesus. And I put them in a book.
If you don't like their rules, whose would you want to use?"[1]

DALE CARNEGIE

FOREWORD

THROUGHOUT MY LIFE I have been fortunate to know many successful and enterprising men and women—in sports, politics, education, business, and life in general. And, I have been helped immeasurably by the writings of so many of these people, many of whom I count as friends.

Jim Floor is one of those people whose example in the business world has been an inspiration to me. In his book, *Throw Away the Crutches,* he captures what is really important in his life—and what should be important in our lives as well. In my years as a professional football player and then as a coach, it was apparent to me that the key ingredients to developing a well-rounded athlete were integrity, discipline, hard work, and perseverance. But since my football years have found that these four character qualities are not just for athletes. They are vital and necessary qualities which must be a part of every person's life if they want to achieve their God-given potential.

When things went so badly for me during the 1988 season, a good friend of mine, former Cleveland Browns' coach Sam Rutigliano, sent me an encouraging note that included this quote from Harry Truman's book *Plainly Speaking:* "The way in which you endure that which you must endure is more important than the crisis itself."

What President Truman was talking about was the need for character. Horace Greeley once said, "Fame is a vapor; popularity an accident. Riches take wing; those who cheer today will curse tomorrow. Only one thing endures—character."

I believe that because I've seen the difference character makes. It was the strength of character that enabled the 1970 Dallas Cowboys to rally after everyone in the country wrote us off and come back to win seven straight games and go all the way to the Super Bowl. It was the great maturity of character that enabled the 1971 team to ignore the controversies and distractions and press on to the goal of becoming Super Bowl champions. I believe it was character that enabled the 1985 Cowboys to play beyond their abilities and win the Eastern Division over two more talented football teams. And it was also character in my final team, the 1988 Cowboys, that enabled them to survive disappointing loss after loss without ever quitting.

I've seen the difference character makes in individual football players, too. Give me a choice between an outstanding athlete with poor character and a lesser athlete of good character, and I'll choose the latter every time. The same with a sales person, an architect, or a teacher. The person with good character will often perform to his or her fullest potential and be successful, while the outstanding sales person, architect, or teacher with poor character will usually fail to perform to his or her potential—and often won't even achieve average performance.

In my opinion, character is the most important determinant of a person's success, achievement, and ability to handle adversity.

These four qualities of character—integrity, discipline, hard work, and perseverance—are qualities that can be cultivated and refined in every person's life. And the building blocks which are outlined in this book can give you the tools, the motivation, and the courage necessary to develop a clear strategy and game-plan for character enrichment and success in your family, your business, and in your personal life.

We had a quote on a sign in our Cowboys' locker room that said, "The quality of a man's life is in direct proportion to his commitment to excellence." What that means is that you have to get up each morning with a clear goal in mind saying to yourself, "Today I'm going to do my best in every area. I'm not going to take the easy way; I'm going to give 100 percent."

Having that kind of commitment doesn't guarantee you'll reach your goals. Some of the time you'll fall short. Occasionally you'll hit an insurmountable obstacle and fall flat on your face. But the determination to strive to do your best will inevitably improve the quality of your life.

The apostle Paul is one of my favorite biblical characters because he was such a competitor. He was beaten, stoned, shipwrecked, and imprisoned, but he never would quit. He explained some of his motivation in a letter to the Corinthian church, saying:

> "In a race, everyone runs but only one person gets first prize. So run your race to win. To win the contest you must deny yourselves many things that would keep you from doing your best. An athlete goes to all this trouble just to win a blue ribbon or a silver cup, but we do it for a heavenly reward that never disappears. So I run straight to the goal with purpose in every step. I fight to win. I'm not just shadow-boxing or playing around. Like an athlete I punish my body, treating it roughly, training it to do what it should, not what it wants to. Otherwise I fear that enlisting others for the race, I myself might be declared unfit and ordered to stand aside."
>
> —1 COR. 9:24-27, THE LIVING BIBLE

Paul understood what it took to be a champion and a successful leader. He realized the quality of a man's life is in direct proportion to his commitment to excellence. That kind of commitment to excellence—the kind of will to win Paul wrote about—is absolutely essential to success in one's life.

We are all indebted to Jim Floor for the wonderful building blocks outlined in his book. It offers hope to those who have lost hope, new possibilities to those who are tired of simply coasting, and a renewed sense of life to those who might feel that life is over.

TOM LANDRY

INTRODUCTION

"The credit belongs to the man who is actually in the arena;
whose face is marred by dust and sweat and blood;
who strives valiantly; who errs and comes short again and again;
who knows the great enthusiasms, the great devotions,
and spends himself in a worthy cause; who at the best knows
in the end the triumph of high achievement; and who at worst,
if he fails, at least fails while daring greatly. . . "[1]
TEDDY ROOSEVELT

WE HAVE FOUND A COMMON denominator among all people, and it is the desire to be fulfilled and successful. This is what most of us fill our time with, expend our energy on, and set our ambitions toward: being fulfilled and successful. There is only one thing more sad than not wanting to be fulfilled and successful: believing that these things are somehow impossible to attain.

We couldn't help but chuckle as we ran across this newspaper article recently:

A man leaped from a fourth-story window and survived by landing on a car, rode an elevator back up and repeated his suicide attempt (jumping from the same window and landing on the same car). The 30-year-old survived both 40-foot leaps, and was in fair condition Sunday at a hospital in Buffalo, police said. . . . In his first attempt Saturday morning, the man dived through a double-paned window, landing on the car, buckling the roof and doors and smashing its rear windows . . . . Although dazed and bleeding from facial cuts, the man got up and walked to the building's elevator, a witness told police. [Police] arrived at the building and saw the man make his second jump onto the crumpled car. The man suffered his most serious injuries in the second fall.

Admit it. You've felt at times that you couldn't even succeed at failing! But it doesn't have to be that way. Our firm conviction is that happiness and success are not out of reach. You simply need to know how to take hold of them.

In this book we talk about crutches as character faults, excuses, and misconceptions which keep us from realizing our full potential. Crutches keep us from being the best we can be, of experiencing the best from life. All of us want to rid ourselves of those pesky character traits and burdens which weigh us down. One of the reasons we find that difficult to do is that we struggle to find the heart of the problem.

Often we only deal with the surface matters rather than with the real issues which are keeping us bound and restricted. This is partially due to the fact that we human beings are incredibly complex creations. Additionally, we live during a time when the pressures of trying to keep up with the fast pace of the 90's can, at times, make life seem overwhelming. As a result, most Americans lead, as Jim has often observed, "lonely lives of quiet desperation." Yet deep down we yearn to attain the happiness, fulfillment and contentment that comes from being successful in various areas of our lives. That success involves spiritual, mental, physical, emotional, psychological, interpersonal, and financial dimensions. With so many factors involved, it is no wonder success is not achieved automatically!

We can liken life in some ways to a championship caliber 400-meter relay team. The team can only expect to win when all four runners are in top form. When one or more runners are struggling, the team won't win no matter how well the others run. The competition is much too strong. Winning in life is much the same. Instead of weak runners, we have identified four character flaws which must be overcome if we are going to truly succeed. They are ignorance, laziness, status, and doubt. Failure to recognize, to admit to, and to convert any of these flaws into strengths will lead to losing in life, no matter how strong we may be in the other areas. The competition is much too strong.

Often without realizing it, we choose to hold on to our limitations, perhaps realizing that without a convenient excuse, we would have to take full responsibility for our lives. When this happens, the character flaw becomes a "crutch," and at best we can only expect to limp through life. We have heard it said, "Argue hard enough and long enough for your limitations, and you will keep them." Our purpose in this book is to help you identify, conquer, and discard the crutches which are hindering you from being the most successful and fulfilled person possible.

IT REALLY IS WITHIN REACH!

Craig and his youngest son, accompanied by their dog Aerial, were recently doing some mountain biking on some country roads near their home. They had just walked their bikes across the highway and onto a dirt road. Craig was about to get on his bike when he noticed Aerial, who was about five feet away, backing slowly down the road. Craig looked up and saw a long and angry-looking snake coiled up in the road. Now, Aerial is the epitome of a city dog. She lives indoors and, to our knowledge, had never seen a snake in her life. She had never read about them, seen a television special on the dangers of snakes, or had her mother hand down stories to her of fights with poisonous vipers.

The begging question is, "How did this consummate city dog know to back up from a snake?" The answer: instinct. She didn't have to be taught to watch for snakes. She didn't have to be reminded to watch her step while out in the woods. She responded naturally. She was naturally gifted to handle the rigors of surviving in the untamed outdoors through her inborn instinct. Wouldn't it be nice if we all had such a natural instinct related to achieving personal success? Yet the truth is that most of us don't. In fact we can often sabotage ourselves and develop habits which hinder us rather than help us.

Happiness and success in life are such important matters that they really shouldn't be left to chance or instinct. Happiness and success happen when you reach your full potential, and we aim to show you how. Success really is within reach. But first you must decide how you are going to live your life. If life were seen as a game, the question you must ask is, "Am I going to play or am I going to play to win?" Life has a great deal to offer you if you are willing to reach out and grab it. Very few people have success handed to them on a silver platter. Your life can surpass your greatest dreams! But first you have to get into the game.

If it were true that some people were destined to be less than their best, we would have no encouragement for you. But we are convinced that such is not the case. William James once said, "Men habitually use only a small part of the powers they actually possess." Researchers today would affirm that we use only a tiny part of the abilities of our brains. We would affirm that ourselves by saying that what God can accomplish through your life is more than you could ever imagine.

We would all like to rid ourselves of our crutches, those things that are holding us back and causing us to fall short of our expectations. Where we most often need help is in identifying specifically what our crutches are and in dealing with the root problems rather than with the symptoms. Like us, you may sometimes find this a painful journey. None of us likes to be confronted with our weaknesses and forced to deal with the basic issues of character. But it is in this process that we can find the only true source of healing and the only road to fulfillment. The great thing about life is that our very weaknesses can be turned into strengths, and our flaws of character can become our greatest sources of strength. To help you in that journey we have attempted to identify the four most common obstacles to personal growth and success, and we have identified some solutions which will allow those of you who are willing to throw away those crutches and to realize your personal potential.

ARE YOU REALLY LIVING?

We live just a short distance from the wide, splendid waters of the San Francisco Bay. On any given weekend, the scenic grandeur of the Bay bears witness to three types of weekend boaters. We'll call the first boater Fred. Fred unloads his 60-foot sailboat into the Bay and pulls directly to the dock, unpacks the ice coolers, picnic baskets, radio, and sunscreen. For the next two days he and his friends talk and frolic on the deck of his romantic sailing cruiser. When he goes into work Monday morning his colleagues ask, "What did you do this weekend?" Fred answers, "I went sailing."

Our second boater we'll name Joe. Joe unloads his 60-foot cruiser into the Bay and pulls directly to the dock, unpacks the ice coolers, picnic baskets, radio, and sunscreen. He and his friends talk and frolic on the deck of his romantic sailing cruiser until Sunday afternoon. Then Joe unties his boat, raises his sails and spends an hour in the waterways of the beautiful San Francisco Bay before he heads for home. When he goes into work Monday morning his colleagues ask, "What did you do this weekend?" Joe answers, "I went sailing."

Our third boater we'll call Pete. Pete unloads his 60-foot sailboat into the Bay, secures the deck, and heads directly through the Bay and into the open waters of the Pacific. He feels the splash of the salt water, navigates through rough waters, feels the exhilaration of the fresh air, and charts his course for two days of adventure on the high sea. When he goes into work Monday morning his colleagues ask, "What did you do this weekend?" Pete answers, "I went sailing."

Who really went sailing? That question is pretty easy to answer. You and I face a similar question. Are you really living or are you tied up at the dock relegated to accepting the situation life has served up to you? Are you really living, or are you simply venturing out for an occasional excursion so you can feel worthwhile? Real life is about challenging the unknown, venturing out into uncharted waters, crossing the boundaries of where you've never been, and stretching yourself beyond your perceived limits. That's real living, and that's the path to reaching your full potential. Let's throw away the crutches. Let's sail!

PART ONE

THE CRUTCH OF
IGNORANCE

Becoming a growing person

"Anyone who stops learning is old,
whether at twenty or eighty.
Anyone who keeps learning stays young.
The greatest thing in life is to keep your mind young."[1]
HENRY FORD

There are many reasons why people fail to achieve what they want from life. The most basic of these reasons often boils down to a simple lack of understanding about how to achieve and what achievement involves. To put it simply, we sometimes fail to achieve out of ignorance. Webster defines ignorance as a lack of knowledge or experience. It is not normally a lack of intellectual capacity which hinders us in our quest for success. Quite to the contrary, Aldous Huxley once said, "Most ignorance is evincible ignorance. We don't know because we don't want to know."

In February of 1891 the British whaling ship *The Star of the East* set out to sea. During the trip, crew member James Bartley tragically fell overboard and was swallowed by a wounded sperm whale. Several hours later the whale was captured. In an amazing example of Providence, reminiscent of the biblical story of Jonah, Bartley was discovered, still alive, in the gigantic stomach of the whale. After recovering, Bartley was interviewed, and he recounted that it had been easy to breathe, but the heat and humidity were terrible. He suffered no lasting injury, although his hair and skin were reported to be permanently changed to white! He was a blessed man to survive such an ordeal. Rarely will we encounter such good fortune in our lifetime. Most often our achievements will be the result of knowing the right road and getting on it.

None of us likes to think of himself as ignorant. It is certainly not a desirable characterization. But if you hope to throw away those crutches which are holding you back from realizing your life's true potential, you must face the question of whether you are falling short of what you could be because of your own failure to understand that success involves three essential components. The first is developing the courage to win. The second is learning the essential skills for making good and wise decisions. And the third is building relationships with people who will be beneficial allies and who will contribute to your success.

CHAPTER

1

DEVELOPING THE COURAGE TO WIN

"All our dreams can come true—if we have the courage to pursue them."[2]
WALT DISNEY

WHY DO WE OFTEN FAIL TO reach our potential? We believe that one of the fundamental reasons is that realizing our potential takes tremendous personal energy and courage. We must develop the courage to win. Never does a person reach his full potential by accident. It is often a long and sometimes even arduous process of self-discovery and personal growth. We are frequently bombarded with difficult decisions and confronted with our own personal flaws. We come face to face with our need for change and even confront demanding questions concerning such vital issues as values, eternity, character, and direction. As a result, we are compelled to ask ourselves some serious questions before we even begin the race toward reaching our potential. The questions are those like: "Do I have what it takes? Can I really achieve all God designed me to be or am I destined to settle for something less than the best? Do I know where I am going and how I will get there?" Facing such questions as these requires courage. There are two foundations which you must build on if you hope to succeed in realizing your personal potential.

FOUNDATION #1

You are responsible for your life

The good news is that you are responsible for your life. Like the baseball team in a contest for the league championship, it is always better to have your destiny in your own hands than to have to depend on another team to win or lose. The bad news is that you are responsible for where you find yourself in life. Though you can get significant help along the way, ultimately you must take the initiative and bear the burden of what you make of your life. All the beneficial effects of a solid family background including a strong system of love and encouragement, quality education, positive experience, and good mentors (as important as they are) cannot replace the simple but profound desire to be the best. We often want to lay blame on others or on our life circumstances as reasons why we have not achieved more in life. And there is no question that many have had to overcome serious obstacles from the past before they were able to move on to the future. But ultimately it is the acceptance of responsibility and the courage to go on that make the difference between success and failure.

We are personally saddened by the glut of statistics which reveal the severe dysfunction many have experienced in childhood and beyond. We've read the heartbreaking story of Ann Jillian, whose phenomenal success as a beautiful and world famous model belied the fact that she had endured a heart-wrenching lifetime of abandonment and unspeakable abuse. The beginnings of her story make one wonder how anyone could recover from such an initiation to life. Unfortunately, the facts tell us that her experience was one which is all too common. But whether we have suffered a similar life tragedy or we've been given every advantage, we can all make the best of what we have. Though we say it with compassion and empathy, the fact still remains that we are all responsible for the willingness, honesty, and courage it takes to go beyond our situation and create a new place in life. It can happen.

History is filled too full with examples of tragic beginnings which lead to happy endings for us to belief anything else. With God's help, we can prevail against any and all odds. The end of Ann Jillian's story is a marvelous example for anyone who has suffered with a past he would just as soon forget. You can never change what has happened to you. But you can affect positively the way your future goes. We will look at some inspiring stories later. For now let us simply say that no matter where you've been, the good news is that you can make the difference in where you go from here.

LIVING WITH COURAGE

Imagine an eloquent and stately man delivering this address to a young and ambitious college graduating class:

Children, you are going to die! One day, sooner than you would hope, they're going to take you out to the cemetery, drop you in a hole, throw some dirt in your face, and go back to the church and eat potato salad! When you were born, you alone were crying, everybody else was happy. The important question I want to ask is this. When you die are you alone going to be happy, leaving everyone else crying?

This might not be a typical address a graduating class would be primed to hear, but his point would be a profound one. What is the legacy that we will leave for those who knew us?

The point of this eloquent pastor's message was a simple but profound one. What is the legacy that we will leave for those who knew us? Will they recite our titles and tell of the good things we did, or will they tell how they are losing a best friend? Will we be known as an anybody or will we be known as courageous? If there is anything that we should want, it should be the peace of knowing that we lived a life that was anything but ordinary. Deep inside all of us there lies a hunger to know that our life had significance. We don't want to be ordinary. The one important and necessary quality that inspires us to succeed at being extraordinary is the character quality of courage. Courage is not simply for the few who face perilous life circumstances. Courage is a quality for all of us.

The best definition we have heard for courage is this: "A purpose or belief, a choice, and an action carried out in support of values . . . despite the known risks." It takes tremendous courage to face the everyday challenges of our lives. Daily we are faced with difficult decisions to do the right thing versus the easy thing, to stick to our convictions or cave in to circumstances, to settle for loneliness or work toward intimacy, to accept our place in life or reach to achieve our real dreams. Courage causes us to stand tall and proclaim loudly, "I don't want to be paralyzed by fear or immobilized by anxiety. I refuse to compromise my convictions or quit difficult challenges. I will not be a coward. I will not be an anybody."

THE COURAGE TO
LIVE BY PRINCIPLE

Everyone lives by principle. Principles are heartfelt beliefs that direct our actions. Principles influence what we do and how we do it. Every action is based on a presupposed belief. Let's take an example. If you believe in the value of honesty in dealing with others, that is a principle. That principle guides the way you deal with everyone from a co-worker to an obnoxious racquetball opponent. Because you believe in honesty in dealing with people, you take the blame when you mess up at work rather than allowing someone else to endure it. Likewise you make the right line call despite the questionable calls your racquetball partner has made himself.

You may think you don't have principles, but you do. You may not be able to delineate or outline what they are, but your life is directed by them anyway. To have no principles is itself a principle. That belief will certainly guide the way you live life. Many have adopted this sort of approach to life: "It's right to live by my word, unless it means personal discomfort. It's right to make the right line call unless that racquetball partner made a blatant bad call last game." While it might sound fair, the person it is most unfair to is oneself. George Washington once said, "I hope I shall possess firmness and virtue enough to maintain what I consider the most enviable of all titles, the character of an honest man." It takes courage to believe and to do the right thing in life no matter what the situation or the consequences. To live by principle is to know what you value in life and to live your life accordingly. Living by principle is about living from the inside out.

INTERNAL VERSUS EXTERNAL MOTIVATION

To really live that kind of life demands that we are internally motivated and not externally motivated. We once heard a legendary story about an exhausted public speaker taking the subway home one rainy Tuesday evening. He had boarded, paid, made his way down the crowded car, and found himself lucky enough to get a seat. Looking at his change he discovered that he had been given too much. While he didn't relish giving up his seat and making the trek back to the front of the car, he did. After returning the change he was surprised to hear the conductor respond, "Thank you. I heard you speak on honesty yesterday, and I wanted to see if you were for real." The public speaker lived by internal motivation. It's not the fear of being caught or the guilt of a bad conscience. It's living in harmony with the values we hold inside.

You've likely had the same experience as us, being given too much change by a store cashier. Craig was once watching a cashier count out what was supposed to be four one-dollar bills in change. The young woman counting back his change obviously didn't see that one of those bills was a ten and not a one. Craig pointed out the error, and the cashier was a little surprised, but grateful nonetheless. The issue here is not whether the money should be returned. The issue is why the money should be returned.

REASON #1: Craig could give the money back because he knows that at the end of the day this cashier will come up short in her cash-drawer count. That nine dollars could put her over the monthly limit, and she could lose her job or be demoted from her position as cashier. That is certainly a possible scenario and a good reason to give the money back. But it is not the best reason.

REASON #2: Craig could give the money back because keeping that extra nine dollars is the same as stealing two spiral notebooks and a ball-point pen. He would be no different than a shoplifter if he kept the money. That is certainly true and this is a good reason to give the money back. But it is not the best reason either.

Each of these options is a result of external motivation. Craig is being motivated by what he perceives as the potential implications of his keeping the money. What's the problem with that? Well, what if the implications change? What if he needed the money to eat that day? What if that cashier were rude to him? External motivation can too easily be rationalized or justified. We need better standards for making our decisions.

There is really only one good reason to give the money back. Craig's action is a direct reflection of what he believes about honesty. Giving the money back is a reflection of what he believes is important in life, his principles. It's in harmony with what he believes. That is internal motivation. It is the only way to live. Internal motivation means that you act because it is the right thing to do, not because you might get caught or be looked down upon by others. This is what it means to live from the inside out. That is what it means to live by principle. That kind of living takes courage.

THE COURAGE TO
LIVE WITH INTEGRITY

How consistent you are with your principles is called integrity. Our place in history has found us hearing a great deal of talk about integrity. Michael Milken, Robert Keating, Jim Bakker, Marge Schott, Michael Irvin, and a host of others have been less than stellar examples of how to live our lives. Life is far too short to live it without being able to feel good about yourself when you put your head on your pillow each night. Integrity is not having to look over your shoulder. It is not worrying whether you'll be caught by a lie you're living or a secret act you've committed. Our dictionary says that integrity is the quality of being whole or undivided. What a vivid way to picture integrity. When you act with consistency upon your values, you are able to live complete. When you fail to live up to your word, to act with honesty, to respond to others consistently, to conduct yourself fairly, you live your life divided. It is impossible to be complete and truly happy living life like that.

Though most of us would believe that, doing it in real life is another matter entirely. We read from Sunshine Magazine, "It's strange that men should take up crime when there are so many legal ways to be dishonest." Indeed you don't have to be a crook to lack integrity, you only have to be an average person. It is alarmingly common to steal "small" items from one's employer or fudge "a little" on the facts. Dishonesty is more common than uncommon in many areas of life. To really live with integrity can often take tremendous courage. In a dog-eat-dog world, how do you win by doing what is right when the other guy isn't? You stay true to the values that guide your life. It's not nearly as difficult when you have a guidebook to follow.

For us that guidebook comes in the form of the Bible. Far from being an ancient book of irrelevant teachings, we have found the Bible to be a highly applicable and inspirational guide for living. Both of our lives are built around it, and the strength that it brings us has made the difference between winning and losing.

THE COURAGE TO EXPLORE YOURSELF SPIRITUALLY

An overwhelming majority of Americans believe in God and agree that we have a spiritual dimension to our lives. We would agree with that as well, and we actually are both committed Christians. One of the things we hear most often among those who aren't believers is the curious concept that faith is for weak people. It is a popular perception that is really quite puzzling since we have found the opposite to be true! The truth is it takes incredible courage to go against the grain of popular practice and say, "I highly value my relationship with God and hold that relationship as my highest priority." Our personal and professional lives are built on a foundation of strong personal faith.

Though many have a vague belief in and concept of God, few people have defined what their faith really means to them or what they base their faith on. Such a widely held belief in God should certainly be something which causes us to reflect seriously on what our spirituality means. We don't know how it could be any other way. If you believe that God is real and that there is an eternity, those are issues which demand exploration. For each of us there was a great deal of soul searching and study that preceded making our faith such a high priority in life, and the Bible played a significant role in that decision. Far from being for weak people, living a lifestyle of faith is for the strong of heart and the sturdy of character.

THE COURAGE TO TAKE RISKS

You will hear us talk often about taking risks. Life is filled with risks, and living is about navigating through a maze of them. Decisions you make concerning health, eating, and exercise involve risk. Decisions to travel and play often involve risk. What we sometimes fail to perceive is that it is a risk to be a high achiever in life. The safest and easiest way to live life is to simply take what life dishes out. But rarely is that going to allow you to reach your potential as an individual. The decision to work toward achieving your personal potential must be an intentional one. It is a risky decision, no question. It is first of all an admission that you haven't obtained all that you can out of your life. Somewhere along the road you have settled for second best. That is a difficult pill for any of us to swallow. More than that, beginning the path to achievement is risking personal disappointment. What if you can't accomplish what you really want? What if you come up short? In truth, it is sometimes easier to avoid the possibility of disappointment than to take a chance of having to deal with its awful burden.

What about you? Will you accept the challenge to embark on a process of self-discovery whereby you can reach your potential? That takes courage. It is not a journey for the timid or the faint of heart. Bravery and fortitude are the prime attributes when it comes to such an important undertaking. To lasso the power of courage for your personal life requires that you undergo a mental transformation, and that is not nearly as mystical as it sounds. It is merely coming to understand the integral part that courage plays in your character. You and you alone are responsible for your life. Even God doesn't assist you as long as you are an unwilling participant. You have to muster the courage to begin that journey. When you understand how much of your happiness in life is determined by courage, you open the door to exciting possibilities.

FOUNDATION #2

You can achieve success

If you are like many people, you really don't worry about whether or not you have reached your ultimate potential. You are more concerned about the fact that you haven't even reached the level of your own expectations. Many of us don't believe that we deserve to win because we are still operating on information that was programmed into our minds in the past like tapes in a machine. We are still looking back at our own failures. We are looking back at the fact that we didn't graduate as valedictorian. We didn't make first string of the football team. We weren't chosen homecoming queen. We were laughed at one time or another. We have a brother or sister who is more successful than we are. We had a parent that was a winner, and we could never measure up. We had a business failure. We were fired from a job. Someone told us we would never make it. Many people don't feel good about who they are, what they have accomplished, or where they are going right now.

Often we sabotage our own success and happiness by living in the past rather than in the present. We continue replaying those tapes over and over in our memory. It's true that if you carry yesterday's baggage into tomorrow, tomorrow won't be any different from yesterday. Many times we simply refuse to forgive ourselves for our mistakes. We will sometimes even look around a crowded room and think better of the people sitting around us than we think of ourselves! All because we are living off tapes from the past. How can we concern ourselves with not reaching our "ultimate potential" when we can't even measure up to our own expectations? The answer is simple but not necessarily easy. Forget the past and move on toward the future. Begin recording a new set of tapes that challenge you to become the best you can be. You can do it. It takes courage, but a foundational element is the belief that you can be a success.

WHAT IS REAL SUCCESS?

Talking about success really compels us to define what we mean by success. Many of us have found ourselves trapped by our understanding, or better yet, our misunderstanding of what success means. Best selling author Dennis Waitley sums it up well in the first chapter of his book, *Being the Best.* "Success is not a destination," he writes, "it is a journey." Success is the process of becoming all you can be and all you should be in each area of your life. Success is realizing your potential in life. With that as an understanding, this book is really all about success. Success is not about money; it is not about power, influence, or fame. Those may or may not be by-products of success. The world is full of people who have gained money and power but don't know happiness. Our conviction is that success begins by building character. Until you have developed character, you will not be able to handle wealth and power (they will handle you). Our intention in this book is not to describe how to build wealth or make money. We have every intention, however, of helping you begin the journey toward real success. Success is knowing what you are becoming and where you are going in life. Success is unwrapping your God-given potential and unleashing it to achieve all that you are capable of achieving. Would anyone want to settle for less?

CAN YOU REALLY BE SUCCESSFUL?

We all have different life goals, ambitions, and dreams. But regardless of what form those dreams and ideas of success take, most of us long for a feeling of significance and yearn to feel that our lives really matter. In fact we can't really be happy unless we are in pursuit of that goal. The brilliant behavioral scientist Abraham Maslow said, "If you deliberately plan to be less than you are capable of being, then I warn you that you'll be unhappy for the rest of your lives." Unfortunately, life can be very cruel, and you may sometimes find yourself battered down until you reach the point where you are willing to accept that an ordinary person like you, with an ordinary life like yours, could never do more than accomplish mere ordinary things. It doesn't have to be that way! It all begins with developing the courage to begin the process of becoming the best that you can be. Can you really be successful? You better believe you can!

CHAPTER

2

LEARNING TO MAKE
WISE DECISIONS

*"Man is man because he is free to operate
within the framework of his destiny.
He is free to deliberate, to make decisions,
and to choose between alternatives."*[1]
MARTIN LUTHER KING

WE HAVE ALL MADE OUR SHARE of bad decisions. How many of us wouldn't love to go back and redo some significant decision in our past. We love the story of the young fourth-grade boy who was called to the principal's office—again. The principal sat down and said with frustration, "This is the fifth time I have had you in my office this week. What do you have to say for yourself?" The little boy wasn't sure how to respond. His uncertain reply was, "I'm glad it's Friday?" It can be a scary thought when we realize that our lives are a sum total of the decisions that we make. We sometimes shudder to think how ill-prepared we often are when we make major life decisions such as who and when to marry, should we have kids, and when, career paths, faith in God, or should I make this major move, and so on. We are a product of our decisions, some major and most minor. The decisions we make and how we make them says as much about us as anything else we do.

Much of the pain that we often blame on God, others, and bad luck is really the result of bad decisions we've made ourselves. Sometimes we forget that God has given us an incredible gift—a multi-billion dollar computer placed right between our ears. However, the ability to make wise decisions is not the product of superior intelligence, and it is certainly not the result of our good fortune. More than anything else, decision-making is a skill that can be learned, cultivated, and developed with an understanding of the right tools. To describe the steps of good decision making almost seems simplistic. There is nothing profound about them, nor are they some new world-shattering discovery. What they are is something all of us need to grasp better and use more.

STEP #1

Get the facts first

We love the wisdom and the directness of the Bible. Certainly many of the Bible's writers were men who lived by the adage, "Say what you mean and mean what you say." This piece of advice is no different: "How stupid . . . to decide before getting the facts!" (PROVERBS 18:13 LB).

That's not too strong of a statement, especially when you consider how often we do exactly what it cautions against. Once when Craig was waiting in a long line for college registration, he got in a conversation with an intelligent-looking student behind him. Somehow in the course of conversation they began talking about the Bible, and this new acquaintance of Craig's had no lack of opinion. "I don't believe in the Bible," he said, "it has too many contradictions." To that Craig just smiled with anticipation. He had talked to this kind of Bible scholar before. "Oh!" was the response, "Where is one of those contradictions?" After a series of "Ah . . . ah's," our pseudo-Bible scholar admitted that he didn't know of any off-hand, but he had heard there were lots of them. What a perfect illustration of making a decision (an important one in this case) based on inaccurate hearsay rather than on the real facts.

Many of our decisions are based on factors other than facts. The average person typically doesn't decide which car to purchase based on quality comparison, driver surveys, annual driving cost statistics, or consumer reports. He likes the way it looks, he likes the sticker price, he likes a particular feature it has, or he likes the image it projects. Though that may or may not come to hurt us in making purchases such as stereos or automobiles, it is a dangerous habit to form when it comes to career choices, relationship decisions, and personal health.

Some of the biggest blunders in decision-making come from merely leaving out pieces of the puzzle. If we are not deciding based upon the facts, on what are we basing our decision? Hearsay? Emotion? Reputation? Those are certainly scary factors on which to base minor decisions, much less major life decisions which will affect us personally, and which may impact our family and countless others with whom we come into contact. Even instinct, a valid tool in making decisions, is something no one would recommend as a substitute for the facts. A little research today can save a lot of heartache tomorrow. With that in mind, you would be wise to accrue a wealth of resources around you that can help you in fact-finding. There is no more valuable resource than books. Be a constant reader, stocking your well of wisdom to be used in making good choices. Relevant magazine articles, tapes, and reports can all become rich fact-based sources that you can use to gather information.

Good decision making requires diligence. There are three types of decisions; you've undoubtedly heard of them. There are win/ lose, and lose/lose, and win/win decisions. The most common type of decision is the win/lose. Option one, you win. Anything else, you lose. It is simple. It is basic. It is primitive. It takes the least amount of thought, but it carries with it great risk. It is a high stakes game, and losing looms large as the consequences of a poor choice. It is certainly not the best alternative.

It would seem puzzling that anyone would choose the lose/lose option, but they do. With this alternative there is really no good out-come. Either choice means a loss. People choose it because they see no other solution. But, there is always a better solution than lose/lose.

The most difficult of all decisions, but easily the best, is the win/win. With the best result, you get the greatest reward. With the alternative outcome, you still get a win. The win/win decision takes time, focus, and energy. Rarely are win/win decisions made without a firm grasp on the facts. Who, what, when, where, and how will this decision have impact. Those are the questions which guide us to discover our win/win decisions. Obviously, the bigger the decision, the more time and energy we put into this discovery process. But this is where good decisions begin.

It is sometimes easier to understand principles when we put

them in terms of a real life illustration. Here is one from Craig which brings the discussion home. Craig's son Micah is a very talented young wrestler. It is a sport which is ideally suited to his small stature. He is aggressive, disciplined, and very athletic. Wrestling is his passion, and he hopes one day to parley his skills into a college scholarship. His early successes demonstrate that such an ambition is no pipe dream, with both a California State and the twelve Western States Regional championship already under his belt.

Micah has also taken a liking to youth football and excelled in that arena as well. The hard reality remains, however, that Micah's future in athletics will not likely be in the arena of football. His family gene pool makes men well under the six-foot mark, and that doesn't bode well for football. He nonetheless enjoys football, and it gives him a break from his practice in wrestling. Now a challenging dilemma presents Micah with an opportunity to use the lose/lose, win/lose, win/win principles. Does he concentrate solely on wrestling where his future is bright and his potential unlimited? Or does he wrestle and also play football for fun, but with that fun, risk possible injury, jeopardizing his wrestling future?

How can we use the above principles to zero in on a good decision? First the lose/lose scenario: Micah wrestles exclusively and does not play football. The problem here is that Micah runs the risk of burning out in wrestling. He could resent wrestling because it stole his opportunity to experience success and fun in youth football as a young athlete. This is not a good choice.

The second scenario is win/lose. Micah gives primary attention to wrestling but still plays football throughout youth and high school. He lessens the risk of burnout in wrestling, but greatly increases his chances of sustaining an injury which threatens his chance to secure a college scholarship. In the event that an injury does occur this decision becomes win/lose. This decision could work but there may be a better option.

Scenario three is the win/win option. Micah gives his primary focus to developing his wrestling skills but finds off-season hiatus in youth football. He plays football in youth league where the risk of injury remains minimal. Then when high school starts and the risk of injury for a small-statured athlete increases sharply, wrestling becomes the sole focus. This could very well be the win/win option which could work for Micah. When we build the habit of filtering our decisions through this analytical process, our ability to make good decisions increases dramatically.

STEP #2

Ask for advice

As crucial as it is to get all of the facts, that is not always the final answer. Facts must be interpreted, and interpreted correctly. It is amazing how different politicians can use the same statistics to prove opposite conclusions. As someone once said, "Figures lie and liars figure." Often different people can see the same facts in different ways. Some studies indicate that simply the way we receive facts can influence how we interpret them. In several case studies of mock juries, various jurors presented with precisely the same facts could be swayed by the order in which the facts were presented. Whatever that might say, the truth is that we can be influenced by perspective, emotions, preconceived ideas, or even the sheer number of facts with which we are forced to deal. We need help in knowing what to do.

How directly can we say this? Okay, here it is. The more informed advice you get, the more likely you are to win. We are often taught to believe that a sign of real strength is the ability to live and act independent of anyone's help. Nothing can be further from the truth or less wise. Whenever you need to make a decision, the questions you should instinctively ask yourself are, "Who can help me? Who has made this decision before? Who has done what I am trying to do?" As a soldier once said, "The best way to get through a minefield is to follow someone who has made it." Life is a minefield made much safer by getting wise counsel.

It is foolish to ignore the wealth of experience all around us from those who have tried and succeeded, and from those who have tried and failed. From each of them you can learn lessons which can help you avoid mistakes and duplicate victories. You increase your own abilities and skills when you can accept good advice from others. One of life's great universities is the school of hard knocks. But while the lessons are good, the tuition is high. You have the choice of enrolling there yourself or of learning from someone who has already attended. Don't simply seek the advice of one person. Get a wealth of input on your situation. The bigger the decision, the more input you should get. You may find it helpful to have a wealth of mentors and friends on whom you can call for input and advice as we do.

Jim can vividly recall when he sought the input of a close and respected friend regarding a business into which he was considering investing his time and resources. This friend gave him strong advice which was the opposite of what he was getting from many other people at the time. Not only did this friend not recommend the investment Jim was considering, he ridiculed it as a viable option. Faced with such strong opposing opinions from various people, Jim was forced to rethink his stance and redefine his thinking. It was a soul-searching time, and Jim's final decision was to invest. Jim did invest, and that business has since prospered. Our point is that important decisions often require a significant investment of time and energy. You are wise if you seek input from a variety of sources and are not afraid of opinions that are different from yours and even threatening to you. Jim's skeptical friend has since become a strong supporter of the venture, and he unwittingly played a major part in the decision to invest. Good decisions are made when you are not blinded by knowing only one side of an issue. Seeking input from others will keep you from making wrong choices that cost you dearly.

As important as it is to get advice, it is equally important to get advice from the right sources. Bad advice is worse than no advice at all. Would you ask your plumber to help you prepare your will, or your mechanic where you should invest your inheritance? Not in many situations is that going to be astute. While you should get input from lots of sources, not all advice is of equal weight. Too often our search for advice is merely a desire for approval. We look to have our decisions verified by finding those who will agree with us or give us permission to do what we want to do anyway.

We once heard of a man who called his counselor to ask if he would go to hell if he divorced his wife. He knew the answer to that question. While God wouldn't send him to hell for it, neither would He be pleased by his abandoning his wife. What this man wanted was for his counselor to back him up in his decision to file for divorce. Such schemes are neither advice-seeking nor honest, because we are not really wanting to do the best thing, but only what we have already resolved to do. Honestly look for advice, consider the source, and carefully weigh the options with all their potential repercussions. Soon you will naturally and instinctively learn to perform these steps in all your decisions.

To play devil's advocate for a moment, we want you to understand that to achieve your potential may sometimes mean flying in the face of popular opinion. Calvin Coolidge is quoted as saying, "I have found it advisable not to give too much heed to what people say when I am trying to accomplish something of consequence. Invariably they proclaim, 'It can't be done.' I deem that the very best time to make the effort." Mary Kay Ash, the founder of Mary Kay Cosmetics, would echo that sentiment. In 1963, she and her husband invested their life savings into their new cosmetics firm. Just a month later her husband died, and she was advised to liquidate the company to salvage at least some of her investment. She said no. Later her accountant told her that she was paying too much commission and that she couldn't succeed without reducing her pay scale. She said no. Today, Mary Kay Cosmetics is one of America's largest and most successful cosmetics firms. Sometimes it not only pays, but it is necessary to press on despite the advice you are given. The average person is often very much against the dreams of the person striving to become the best he can be.

Be careful, however, when you fail to heed advice from good sources whom you trust. Over time, as you get advice, you will learn who gives wise counsel. Lean on those people who have a track record of success, and be assured that whether or not you follow their advice, you will always learn, and you will always be ahead by seeking good advice.

STEP #3

Prepare for the worst

We're not talking doom and gloom when we say that part of good decision-making is preparing for the worst. We are simply describing the logic of thinking your decision through. Part of thinking your decision through is considering the potential challenges your decision could create. It is through this process that you can actually avoid problems before you have to live with them. It is much easier to deal with a potential problem than to deal with the problem itself once a bad decision has been made. It is sometimes difficult or even impossible to reverse decisions that have already been tallied and recorded in the score book.

In the Bible, Jesus describes a proud man who set out to build a house. We can imagine that with enthusiasm and painstaking attention to detail he designed his blueprint. He very carefully laid the foundation. With precision he raised the frame and proceeded forward. Suddenly the unexpected happened. He ran out of money. His project came grinding to a halt, and he found himself in the unenviable position of being the laughingstock of the city. People jeered and secretly applauded the fall of the pompous developer. But worse than the ridicule was the fact that he was faced with the loss of his house and, worse still, the loss of his dream. Why did it happen? Because the builder failed to calculate whether he had enough capital to finish the job before he started it. The point of Jesus' story was that we should be careful to always count the cost. Certainly we would want to follow the same precautions in our life decisions.

"How could a developer make such a stupid mistake?" you might ask, and rightly so. But the real question is, "How do we avoid similar mistakes?" Why do we leave a trail of unfinished business ventures, only to later find "it wasn't for me?" Why do we so glibly embark on marriage and so casually add children to the equation, only to say later "we can't make it work?" Rather than counting the cost and determining "what will make it work," we often would prefer a naive optimism that is going to "just believe it will work!" That sort of optimism is neither useful nor optimistic.

Eleanor Porter wrote a novel about the infamous Pollyanna, who wasn't optimistic, but just foolish. Time and time again she refused to face the facts. Decision-making is no place for Pollyannas.

Decision-making requires careful preparation and thought-fulness. You will need to ask yourself some tough questions: "Am I willing to give what this will cost in time, energy, and money? What are the advantages and disadvantages of this decision? Who will this affect? Am I willing to stretch myself? What are the possible outcomes of this decision? What is my course of action in each situation? What am I willing to do to make this work?" While such questioning and planning should become a natural part of your inner process of decision-making, that should in no way lead you to an equally devastating mistake of becoming paralyzed and avoiding any decision at all. We shouldn't try to fool ourselves. We can never prepare for every surprise. To make a decision is to take a risk.

The writer of Ecclesiastes said, "If you wait for perfect conditions, you'll never get anything done." But when we ask the right questions we will have less chance of being surprised by what should have been avoidable. None of us is innocent of failing to calculate the cost of our unwise decisions or our inability to follow through with a commitment. Certainly, we will want to make that sort of evaluation a part of our future decision-making process.

STEP #4
Expect the best and do it

Once you have done the proper research by gathering the facts, getting input, and preparing for problems, you are ready to follow through with your decision. When it comes to making the decision, your attitude is key. William James said, "Men can alter their lives by altering their attitude." You need to be able to conclude with confidence that you have done your best in preparation and that you are confident that you are making the right choice. Now is the time for optimism and enthusiasm. Now is the time to expect with full faith that the plans you have made will work. It is this optimism that will carry you through when the average person would quit. It is this enthusiasm that keeps you going when the ordinary person would drop out.

Jim has warm memories of the power of optimism. They swirl with autumn winds and resound with the echo of shoulder pads and pigskin. Jim's son, Andrew, was only thirteen years old and was the star running back on his youth football team for which Jim was an assistant coach. It was a semi-final playoff game against the undefeated Sacramento Vikings. The winner of the game would go on to play the champion of the Bay Area for the Northern California championship.

The Vikings intimidated and dominated everyone they faced. They were a well-coached inner city team filled with a roster of immensely talented and athletic players. Andrew's team, the Roseville Bobcats, was a well-disciplined and talented team in their own right. They rarely made mistakes and brought with them a great winning tradition. It was set to be a great match-up between these two perennial powers. The stands were packed with fans for both sides. It was an electric atmosphere, and anticipation was high.

The game didn't start out well for the Bobcats. They dug themselves a hole beginning with the opening offensive play. Their quarterback dropped back to pass and was intercepted. The Vikings returned the ball to the five-yard line and proceeded to score a touchdown. To make matters worse, the quarterback was lost to a shoulder injury. Things seemed bleak for the Bobcats when two additional turnovers led to scores. When halftime arrived they found themselves down by a score of 19-0.

Leaving the field for halftime, Jim was talking to Andrew about how the Bobcats would come back in the second half. Andrew's response was, "Dad, they're kicking our tails." Andrew wasn't the only one who was discouraged. The players were grumbling, the other coaches were angry, and spirits were sinking fast. Jim was the last one to speak to the team before heading out for the second half. In his three-minute talk Jim outlined his vision for the second half. They would hold the Vikings scoreless the second half, score four touchdowns themselves, and win the game. No one would be left with a question of who the better team was. Above all, they would do their best because they were not quitters!

Back on the field the Vikings were sent reeling when Andrew took a swing pass and scampered fifty-five yards for a touchdown. However, a clipping penalty erased that score. Undeterred, the Bobcats again drove down the field and scored on a two-yard touchdown run by Andrew. The extra point was missed, so the score was now 19-6. Life was back in the Bobcat team, and they began to surge with a new-found confidence. A defensive stop gave their offense the ball again, and an early fourth-quarter drive was capped by a thirty-yard touchdown run by Andrew. Again the extra point was missed, so the score was now 19-12. The Vikings were now visibly shaken. Worry was written across the faces of the Viking coaches, and the players were beginning to lose their composure.

The Bobcat defense again came up big, making an interception as the Vikings were threatening a score of their own. The game came down to one final and dramatic drive with the Bobcats holding the key to their own destiny. A twenty-five-yard pass completion. A forty-five-yard screen play. Thirty seconds remained in the game, and the Bobcats stood on the two-yard line and faced a fourth-down play. The back-up quarterback dropped back and found the tight end open in the end zone. Touchdown! The score now: Vikings 19, Bobcats 18. The Bobcats lined up for the extra point kick. In youth football the kick, if successful, counts two points because it is considered more difficult than to run or pass. The kicker had been nearly perfect all year long. But this time he didn't even get a chance. The holder fumbled the ball. The game was over and the Bobcats came up short... on the scoreboard. The team that had prided itself on not making mistakes had made virtually every mistake possible.

The Vikings won the game on the football field, but Andrew and his team won a great lesson in life. Attitude can make all the difference between winning and losing. Enthusiastically expecting the best can carry you through the most difficult situations. This lesson was one which Andrew carried through the rest of his high school career. His was a great career which included a State Championship, all-time leading rusher for his league, League MVP, first team All-State of California, Blue Chip All-American, and Division I Scholarship recipient. Andrew learned just how much attitude can make the difference in our successes and failures. It often separates winners from losers.

It is important that you don't allow preparation for decision-making to paralyze you. It is easy to become dazed by the immensity of difficult situations, and you can sometimes make wrong decisions by making no decision at all. You may even seek to avoid failure by postponing a decision until it is decided for you. To fail to make decisions is to decide that you will take whatever life dishes out to you. It is to allow circumstances to make your decisions for you, and rarely will that work out to your benefit. The following story has been ascribed to Dr. Suess. It is a powerful lesson about the need to make a strong decision.

> *Did I ever tell you about the young Zoad who came to two sides in the fork in the road. He looked one way and the other way too, so the Zoad had to make up his mind what to do. Well the Zoad scratched his head and his chin and his pants and he said to himself, "Now I'll be taking a chance. If I go to place one that may be hot, so how will I know if I'll like it or not? On the other hand though I'll feel such a fool if I go to place two and find that's too cool. In that case I may catch a chill and turn blue. Place one may be the best, not place two. On the other hand though if place one is too high, I may get a terrible ear ache and die. On the other hand though if place two is too low, I might get some terrible pain in my toe. So place one may be the best," and he started to go, and he stopped and he said, "On the other hand though, on the other hand, other hand, other hand though," and for thirty-six hours and one half that Zoad made starts and made stops at the fork in the road, saying "No, don't take a chance, you may not be right." Then he got an idea that was wonderfully bright. "Play safe," cried the Zoad. "I'll play safe. I'm no dunce. I'll simply start off to both places at once." And that's how the Zoad who would not take a chance, got nowhere at all with a split in his pants.*

At some point you simply have to do it. Make the decision. Plunge in and expect the best.

There is no mystery surrounding the making of wise decisions. It is a process of learning the right principles and applying them where they are needed. This is certainly one of the most important factors for success. If you are to reach your potential, good decision-making is a skill that is indispensable.

CULTIVATING YOUR CSQ
(COMMON SENSE QUOTIENT)

At this point, it is vital that you understand the distinction between intellectual capacity and what we like to call good old-fashioned common sense. Making good decisions often has little to do with intelligence. There are lots of people who know lots of information, but who make a habit out of making bad decisions. Knowledge doesn't make someone a good decision-maker. What makes a good decision-maker is the application of knowledge. That is what we call common sense. We all know people who have never been to college, but who are known for making wise decisions. They have loads of common sense that no amount of education can buy. Common sense asks the right questions, looks beneath the surface, and learns from the past.

In many ways, this is an exciting time to be alive. We are more fortunate than anyone who has lived before us throughout history. No one has had access to more information, more facts, more data, more news, or more knowledge than we do right now in the time we are living. Not only is all of this information out there, but technology makes it available to all of us. It is almost staggering to see how fast technology is advancing and knowledge is increasing. Some reports indicate that the amount of information is doubling every five years. Each day we awake to national news programs that update us on the latest events in our turbulent world. We browse over our daily newspaper, checking the opening stock prices and the scores of yesterday's ball games. Do you realize that one copy of a daily newspaper from one of our major cities contains more information than you would have encountered in an entire lifetime, had you lived in seventeenth-century England? We exchange our information constantly as we rifle out faxes, talk in our share of over 1.3 billion daily telephone conversations, and read (or throw away) our share of 400 million pieces of daily mail. Our lives are becoming a frenzy of facts, and the ironic thing is that psychologists tell us that within twenty-four hours we forget up to eighty percent of the information that comes our way.

It is certainly no wonder that it is becoming more and more difficult to make decisions. After all, when many of us were kids, choosing our flavor of ice cream from the parlor was easy. We could have vanilla, chocolate, or strawberry. Today, we have to first decide between frozen yogurt and ice cream, then between fifty-two flavors of each! We could have been born in fifteenth-century Europe when we would have never traveled more than fifteen miles from the place we were born, and where we would have died in a world that was basically the same as the one in which we had been born. But instead, God has put us in an age of incredible change and sometimes mind-boggling complexity. To navigate our times requires some skill.

DECISIONS AND COMMON SENSE

Common sense is a capacity that can be acquired. The Bible calls it wisdom and devotes an entire book (the Book of Proverbs) to discussing what it is and how to apply it. One Bible writer, James, says that it is such a valuable commodity that to find it should be viewed as an essential ingredient to life. We should each long for it and ask God to give it to us. It is a pearl of great price and an uncut gem. With it all of our knowledge becomes usable and meaningful. With it we hold the key to unlocking the mystery behind many of life's confusing decisions. With wisdom we are able to see God at work in our lives. Without it we relegate those same events to coincidence. With wisdom we are able see past the surface to discover the real issues confronting us. Without it we are left reeling by events we can seemingly never understand.

Wisdom. Yearn for it. Study it. Ask about it from people you know who have it. Ask God for it. Most of all, obtain it and use it.

WHEN WE MAKE A BAD DECISION

We know of no one who at some time or another has not made a bad decision. All the fact-finding, advice-getting, advanced preparing, and optimistic doing will not change the fact that you will sometimes make bad decisions. Everyone does. We have. You will. When you operate in the business world as Jim does, speculation and educated gambles are a part of life. When an investment goes sour, you try to keep it in perspective. When Jim has lost money he will often say to himself, "Okay. It's not the end of the world; it's only money. This is an opportunity to bounce back." That's opportunity for us to discuss a great question. What do we do when a bad decision has already been made?

One way or another, you have to deal with the results of the decision that was made, even when it is a bad one. First ask, "Is there any way to reverse this decision?" We once knew a young man who found himself on a new car lot looking at the sports car of his dream. The only problem is that it was about twenty-five thousand dollars over what he needed to spend on a car. Nevertheless, our friend found himself driving home in the exhilarating seat of his brand new turbo-charged sports car. It was a simple matter of about two days before he realized the serious damage his purchase had inflicted on his family budget. Can a decision like that be reversed? You never know. Maybe trading that car in now will cost some money, but not as much as repossession will eighteen months down the road. While it is certainly better to make a good decision up front, we should survey our options at every point when decisions have gone sour.

If a decision can't be reversed, ask yourself "What are my options at this moment? How can I live with my decision now? Are there any alternatives I can explore?" In the turbulent world of real estate, recouping losses is a fact of life. When the Sacramento housing economy was hot, Jim had purchased some property and subdivided it to build five starter homes. He built three and kept two lots for reserve. Two of the homes sold quickly, but one stubbornly remained unpurchased. An unoccupied home is an income robber for numerous reasons. Then the economy turned sour, house prices plummeted, and little hope was left for selling this one remaining house. Months went by with the house unoccupied, and soon vandals began to have their way. Someone even stole the garage door! Something had to be done. Jim learned that a friend was struggling. He had lost his job and his home. Jim was able to offer him a rent-free place to live, and his friend was able to occupy, repair, and maintain the unsold house until it could be sold. While it may not always turn out that well for you, you can usually make a positive out of just about any situation. Still, your bad decisions can sometimes exact payment from you for a long time. You will sometimes have to live with the those effects until they play themselves out.

Other times, circumstances can be blessings in disguise. Sometimes great discoveries are formed out of bad decisions. There is even a word for that. It is called serendipity. Serendipity is "accidentally" making fortunate discoveries. Look for the silver lining. You could have stumbled onto the best thing under the sun. You certainly won't know until you look. Even if that doesn't turn out to be the case, you can still try to salvage what you can from the situation. How can you make the best out of where you are? That you've made a bad decision is no reason to give up. Keep laboring and make the best of that with which you are left to work.

It almost sounds trite, but it is unmistakably true. The best thing you can do after a bad decision is learn from it. Try to determine how and why you made the decision. Was there faulty logic? Did you fall to an emotional reaction? Did you use short-term thinking which was not tied to long-term goals? How can you avoid a similar error in the future? Often it is through this process that we cultivate our common sense and learn to make good decisions in all areas of life. It is a useless tragedy that many people make mistake after mistake because they never learn from the past. We have seen countless spouses suffer the misery of a broken relationship, only to fall right back into another one to experience the same anguish again. Psychologists tell us that most partners of failed marriages will experience the same failure in future relationships. All of this pain could have been avoided by simply taking the time and energy to learn from past mistakes and bad decisions. Regardless of what that costs in time and emotion, it is a small price to pay.

Nothing can take the place of making wise decisions. Sooner or later the inability to do the right thing will spell the difference between success and failure. But don't fear. You too can become known for making wise decisions. Soon people will be coming to you and asking advice for the decisions they are facing. Learning and practicing these principles will put you on the fast track toward success.

3

BUILDING BENEFICIAL RELATIONSHIPS

"Union gives strength."[1]
AESOP (THE BUNDLE OF STICKS, 550 BC)

SOMEONE HAS SAID, "I'D rather have a million friends than a million dollars, for if I ever did get hard up, I know I could at least count on a dollar from each." There is nothing more priceless in all of life than good friends. A strong network of friends has the unique distinction of benefiting everyone involved. We need friends for numerous reasons. We'll see many of those reasons in this important chapter.

THE UNIVERSAL NEED
FOR RELATIONSHIP

The desire for intimacy and relationship is one of our most distinguishable characteristics as humans. From the screaming infant who can only be calmed by the loving touch of his mother, to the awkward adolescent who struggles to know how he relates to his contemporaries, to the grandfather who finds such joy in seeing the face of a grandchild to whom he has just given a gift, people exhibit an intense desire to share warm moments of love and friendship with others. The driving force is more than a desire, however. We have a universal need for relationships and intimacy with other people. Numerous studies illustrate the fact that if we lack significant amounts of love, affection, and touching, especially as young children, we will become emotionally scarred.

The University of Miami Medical School has a touch research department which conducted a study on touch and its impact on prematurely born babies. Traditional wisdom held that touching these at-risk preemies would cause great stress and risk illness. To test this presumption, the researchers took twenty of the newborns on the premature ward and gave them three daily fifteen-minute massages. The results were dramatic. Within ten days the massaged babies had gained forty-seven percent more weight than their non-massaged ward-mates. Months later they displayed greater mental and physical skills and were able to leave the hospital an average of one week earlier. A lifetime of touching, building and developing meaningful relationships is a natural and intricate part of being human.

The happiest people alive are those who have cultivated strong relationships with friends who can build them up. It is not enough to have companions; you need true friends with whom you can share your dreams, your joys, your failures, and your insecurities. You were created with a need to relate in that way to others, and to God. Without relationships of both kinds, you will experience a great void and emptiness which cries out to be filled. Truly you will be crippled, and it will limit your potential for real achievement and success.

FRIENDS ARE A REFLECTION
OF OURSELVES

Friends do more than fulfill a deep-seated need for relationship. Our friends reveal a great deal about who we are. We sometimes say jokingly, "Be careful who you spend your time with, because you will one day look just like them!" Although that doesn't exactly thrill our wives, it is a truth that has been known for centuries. A well-known proverb states that, "a mirror reflects a man's face, but what he is really like is shown by the kind of friends he chooses."

If you want to know where you will be in five years, just look at the people you are spending most of your time with today. That is a telling indicator of the future. To say that it is important to build a network of people around you who would reflect your values, goals, and ambitions is something of an understatement. It is not just important; it is paramount. Your friends are more powerful influences on you than you might imagine. While you are not exactly a helpless victim of the environment in which you find yourself, you are more likely to fall prey to your environment without an intentional effort on your part. Let's just say that your friends can be your greatest asset or your most notable liability.

So just ask yourself: "With whom do I most enjoy spending

time? In whom do I confide? What are the values and priorities of those I am with most often? What are the goals and ambitions of my friends?" If you don't like the answers of these types of probing questions, you may want to build some new allies around you. It doesn't take a lot of friends to make a difference, just a few really good ones.

HOW TO FIND
GOOD FRIENDS

The University of Connecticut conducted a study to determine what kind of people made the best friends. It is interesting to note that those people who were found to be the most well-liked and popular often shared a common trait. The one most commonly noted feature was that they demonstrated the greatest capacity to trust others in their relationships. What a lesson! While most of us typically notice such factors as personality, looks, and status, the facts indicate that being a good friend is the key to getting good friends. What a novel concept. Want to find good friends? Be a good friend yourself. Respond to people in your life with consistency and character. Live by your word and always follow through on a promise. These are the qualities that we find attractive in our friends because they help build trust. Good friends have good friends. Friends are not objects which we manipulate and use for our own self-improvement. Friends are people in whom we can invest ourselves and from whom we can benefit.

You undoubtedly need the relationship, the support, the intellectual stimulation, and the personal growth that comes from good friends with whom you share common values. There is power in associating with friends who share common dreams and aspirations. But the paradox of real friendship is that you get those benefits only when you give them away first. The quality of your friendships will only be as strong as the depth of your giving to others. The characteristics that you would want and need in your friends are the very characteristics that you will also want to work on in yourself. Here are a few of those attributes on which to build your network of mutually encouraging friends.

FRIENDS BUILD EACH OTHER UP

Have you heard about the mother watching her son pitch at his first baseball game? She didn't know much about baseball. You couldn't have convinced her that after five innings her son was being pummeled and his team humiliated. She turned to the embarrassed father of the shortstop who was sitting below her on the bleachers and said, "Isn't my son a great pitcher? He hits that bat no matter how the players hold it!" We could all benefit from that kind of encouraging person in our lives. If there is anything that our network of friends should do, it is to encourage us. Do your friends build you up or do they simply give you "reality checks?" You need to be told that you can do it. You need to know that you have friends who believe in you. If your friends won't do it, who will?

FRIENDS SEE THE BEST IN EACH OTHER

We need to be told what we can be and not what we are right now. As Johann Wolfgang Von Goethe said, "Treat people as if they were what they ought to be, and you help them become what they are capable of being." Do you have friends who see the best in you? Do your friends affirm the potential which is lurking just below what the average Joe sees? When I see my friend who is not motivating his children well, I can try to influence him in two ways. I can tell him what a lousy father he is and dump on him all the things he is doing wrong. Or, I can tell him what a great father he could be and possibly suggest some of the things he can do to improve. Encouragement tends to give us something to live up to which is positive, and disapproving criticism tends to give us something to live down to which is negative. We are all much more motivated by positive encouragement than by negative criticism.

Unfortunately, you may have someone in your life who acts as your personal "Lucy." Everyone knows Lucy in the Peanuts comic strip by Charles Schulz as the not-so-encouraging friend of Charlie Brown. Charlie Brown is the consummate loser. Poor Charlie Brown never seems to do anything right, and with friends like Lucy there's no wondering why! One cartoon strip we saw went something like this: "You [Charlie Brown] are a foul ball in the line drive of life. You stand in the shadow of your own goal post. You are a miscue. You are three putts on the 18th green. You are a 7-10 split in the 10th frame. You are a missed free throw and a shanked nine iron. You are a called third strike. You are a dropped rod and reel in the lake of life. Do you understand me, Charlie Brown? Have I made myself clear?" None of us needs that type of personal influence in life.

What we really need is a Barnabas, whose name is translated "Son of Encouragement." Who was Barnabas? He was known in the early church as a "son of encouragement" because of the way he lifted up people around him and made them become better. Barnabas was like the pro athlete described as "making everyone around him a better player." Friends should be like that. They should make each other better. Our friends should expect the best of us because we will rise to the occasion. That is what we need personally, and that is what we should strive to be like for others.

Sometimes you may feel that it is difficult and time-consuming to encourage people on a regular and consistent basis. That is really not the case at all. Steven Duck, in his book *Friends for Life,* asked a group of people to recall the most important phone calls they had received that day. He found that the most important calls weren't long "meaning of life" conversations. The most important ones they got were two-to-three-minute calls from friends that consisted of simple conversations like, "I've been thinking about you." "Good luck in your interview. You can do it." "How are things going today?" That's what friends do for each other. It doesn't require lots of time. It doesn't demand degrees in behavioral science. It might simply involve a well-placed smile, a thoughtful note, or a quick but considerate phone call. Do those things for others, and you will not likely have a shortage of encouraging friends who are doing the same for you.

HOW TO HANDLE CRITICAL PEOPLE

But you may be thinking, "What do I do about the Lucys in my life?" That's a good question, and one which we need to discuss. You really have two choices. On the giving end you may need to take the offensive and simply say, "Quit!" Sometimes Lucys need to be told to knock it off, that you aren't going to put up with it any more. Often negative and fault-finding people have developed a habit of criticism that they don't even recognize. Critical people are often people who are hurting themselves. Whenever Jim has to deal with someone regarding an unpleasant topic, he will often say, "I care enough about you to share the truth, even at the risk of my popularity." Sometimes confrontation is the only way to let them know how unproductive and destructive they are being. We always encourage a loving and humble attitude when confronting hurtful, critical people. The Bible advises telling the truth to others in a spirit of love. A transparent and sincerely loving attitude which highlights specific instances of the hurt you have experienced may open the doors to a healing process for both parties. Compassion and tactful firmness are usually your best allies in any type of personal confrontation.

There are times, however, when taking the next step is called for. We may need to do our best to limit our exposure to Lucys who won't come around to a more loving, encouraging attitude. We certainly would see this as a last resort. Limiting your exposure to important people in your life also limits your ability to impact them towards positive change. You may become an indispensable and influential friend to Lucy. You may be the best friend Lucy has, and to abandon her would be tragic. Jesus said that we should all be salt, influencing others positively. You can't positively influence someone whom you have deserted. Nonetheless, limiting your exposure to certain people is sometimes a difficult but necessary step to take.

Reality also proves that there will be times and situations when it can be difficult or impossible to remove yourself completely from the effects of negative people. Sometimes that negative person is a spouse, a boss, or a family member. When there are unavoidable people in your life that drag you down, all is not lost. You have the option of countering the criticism by cultivating a support group that can soften the blow of those negative influences on you. That support group may be a number of like-minded persons sharing the same career goals, similar growth or recovery needs, or corresponding beliefs and value systems. By spending significant amounts of time with these like-minded people, you can bring balance to your life and offset the negative influences of Lucy. These like-minded friends will keep you constantly reminded of where you want to be, and what you are working to become.

FRIENDS CHALLENGE
EACH OTHER TO GROW

Friends must do more than blow sunshine in our ears. Criticism is not a bad word. It is simply the art of finding areas of weakness as well as areas of strength. Criticism offered constructively is a valuable commodity. As important as encouragement is, our relationships require more than simply positive feedback. Relationships of depth often require honesty. We often need improvement, and who will help us do that if not our friends? Nothing can replace the well-placed words of friends who are interested in building us up without trying to tear us down in the process.

Johnny Carson reigned as the king of late-night comedy television for over two decades. When he was succeeded by his friend Jay Leno, it was a momentous event. But the beginnings of Johnny and Jay's relationship wasn't what you might expect. After seeing Leno's act at *The Comedy Store,* Johnny spoke to him, saying, "You seem like a very funny young man, but you don't have enough jokes." Leno was devastated. Later he recalled, "When I watched the Carson show I saw him do fifteen or twenty jokes. I realized I'd been doing only three and relying on clowning and gestures for the rest of the laughs." He continued, "I resented what Johnny had said, but I took it to heart and began honing my material. A few years later, Carson asked me on his show. I'll always be grateful to him for giving me real advice." Be aware. People can always intuitively tell whether you have their best interests at heart. When you do, a well-placed piece of advice, given with the right motives, is priceless.

One of the most helpful pieces of advice we have received regarding criticism is what we call the sandwich approach. When giving criticism to someone, couch it between two positives. Find a positive encouragement on the front end. Share your constructive criticism. Then wrap it up with a positive on the back end. But beware! To do that demands immense energy. Most of us are geared to see the negatives and often must work against our nature to find two praises for every criticism. But the energy spent is well worth it. People will know that you care. They will understand that you want what's best for them and aren't simply trying to tear them down. It is a gift we would want from others and a gift we should offer to others.

FRIENDS HOLD EACH OTHER ACCOUNTABLE

Friends hold each other accountable. If you don't have a group of people who are keeping you accountable for reaching your goals, for developing your personal life, for honing your skills, for making and keeping your commitments, and for maintaining your spiritual life, it is quite likely that you won't develop your personal life, hone your skills, make or keep your commitments, or maintain your spiritual life. We can say with certainty that a study of history and people reveals that you won't do any of those things as well alone as you could have with the help of friends who will hold you to your commitments.

We all need friends who will hold us accountable. We can never become on our own what we can with the help of others. Do you have friends who would tell you if they thought you were making a big mistake? Are there people in your life who are aware of your personal goals and will challenge you to get on the ball? Do you have people to whom you have issued an open invitation to give you honest feedback and input? Without those types of relationships, you are only cheating yourself and compromising your ability to reach your potential. We are made to relate to others, and how valuable it is to have friends to whom we can relate with that sort of depth, honesty, and commitment

GUIDELINES FOR CORRECTING OTHERS

Be aware, however, that there are guidelines for this kind of honesty among friends. Never, never correct a friend until you have proven first that you are open to correction yourself. Some people have a "gift" for finding the faults in others, but can't take criticism themselves. A wise friend will ask himself, "How would I respond to someone confronting me about this?" "How can I best bring this up to encourage my friend to look at this candidly and not get defensive?" "Could there be something going on here that I don't know about?" "Am I angry and simply blaming others?" "Do I have the best interests of my friend in mind, or am I looking to build myself up?"

Criticism for some people is a means of making themselves feel better. By finding faults in others they become less focused on their own faults. For others criticism is a way of showing how much they know and making themselves known. We call this the Cliff Claven Syndrome. Cliff was the annoying bar fly in the hit comedy "Cheers." Cliff felt so insecure, and so bad about himself, that he became a know-it-all and habitually tore down others as his way of living with himself. We are able to laugh at a character like that, but all too often we are guilty of doing the same things. Be certain that you are not trying to build yourself up through your criticism of others. You will want to correct your friends. But you should be certain that it is truly for their benefit and not somehow for your own welfare.

It is also important that you remember only to correct your friends in private and not in public. Friends don't do power plays, and a public place is not the forum for correcting, criticizing, or confronting. There is nothing more embarrassing or annoying than to see a husband, wife, mother, father, friend, or anyone else for that matter, read the riot act to someone in public. Everyone is uncomfortable with those displays of inappropriate criticism. It not only does no good, it will normally backfire by building hostility and bitterness. No one likes to look bad, and friends and family should make each other look good. Make a habit of complimenting your friends in public. When there is a need for critique, be sure it is done discreetly and in private. Not only is it just polite, it's much more likely to work!

Solomon said, "Open rebuke is better than hidden love! Wounds from a friend are better than kisses from an enemy!" (PROVERBS 27:5-6). There is only one thing greater than being a friend with that kind of love. It is being a friend who can handle that kind of love.

FRIENDS FORGIVE
EACH OTHER

We often see friendships which have been torn apart and destroyed by some petty quarrel or a simple lack of communication. If you have had many friends at all, you have seen the destructive power of miscommunication and misunderstanding. All of us have been hurt by others. If the truth were told, we have also done our share of hurting others. Some of that hurt was intentional, but most was probably not.

Much of the reason for misunderstandings is that language and communication are imperfect and inaccurate ways of relating to each other. For instance, we have common words that carry different meanings entirely. Other words have delicate shades of similar meanings depending on the context. We might want to use a word that would have dozens of synonyms or closely related words. To complicate it even further, we communicate not just through what we say and do but through how we say and do it. Each minute we send thousands of messages to each other both verbally and nonverbally. Some studies indicate that the majority of our communication is nonverbal. The slight movement of a hand, the posture of your body, the tenseness of your muscles, the subtle movements of your eyebrows, the slight variations of intonation in your voice are all of these things and countless others go into our communicating with others. It's no wonder that communication is such a difficult task. It is challenging even in the best of circumstances. Sometimes, though, we just do stupid things! We say what we don't mean and wish we could take words back. We do things that even confuse ourselves. We can hurt people we never intended to hurt in ways we never anticipated.

51

That is both the tragedy and the reality of being human and having relationships. Relationships can be a messy business and there must be some method for cleaning up. Thus, the importance of forgiveness.

FORGIVENESS BENEFITS EVERYONE

We will always be hurt by other people. That is inevitable. The normal course of action for us is to become thin-skinned and hard-hearted. When we are thin-skinned we are easily offended. Our feelings can be hurt quickly and we become increasingly intolerant of criticism, even when it is genuine and helpful. Because we are so easily hurt our heart becomes hard. We grow to be unforgiving and our primary concern is for our own feelings and not the feelings of others.

Life is much more enjoyable when we reverse the situation. We discover freedom when we work toward being thick-skinned and soft-hearted. When we are thick-skinned we are not easily offended. Instead we are patient with people and we don't react to others negatively. When we live in this way, our hearts can stay soft and pliable. We can forgive others and more easily think of others above ourselves.

True maturity is learning to move beyond our hurts and heal broken relationships. True maturity is learning how to forgive. Forgiveness is releasing the need to "make payback." It is releasing the hurt and restoring a relationship. You will likely never be able to establish a network of real friends until you learn the art of forgiveness. For when we fail to forgive we build a wall of callousness around us. With each ensuing occasion of failing to forgive that calloused wall around our hearts becomes thicker. It is more and more difficult to allow anyone to get close to us.

This is an emotional issue for many. For some, the hurts they have experienced make it difficult to consider embracing forgiveness as a helpful ally. Few who have really been hurt would say that forgiveness is easy. Many, though, would testify that it is worth the price. If ever there was a win/win situation, forgiveness is an illustration of it. It breaks down the walls. It allows for new beginnings. It heals.

FORGIVENESS FREES YOU FROM THE DAMAGING EFFECTS OF BITTERNESS

If you allow bitterness and resentment to build inside you, you are wrecking the very house that you live in. Your ability to trust, to build deep relationships, or to inspire confidence will be greatly crippled. Soon your ability to make and keep friends will fail. You will find it difficult to establish intimacy, even impossible to move beyond superficiality. Plain and simple lack of forgiveness affects your personal relationships today. Rather than inflicting punishment on the offending party by withholding forgiveness, you inflict it on yourself and on all those other innocent ones who know you, or would benefit from knowing you. To deny this is to spurn the documented cases of thousands of marriage counselors, behavioral scientists, pastors, and friends. Failing to forgive kills.

You may think that forgiveness as a concept is okay. But maybe there is one person you just can't forgive. Let's clear up one misconception. Forgiveness never condones the actions of an offending party. It never accepts a wrong that has been done. Forgiveness simply moves you from the pain of the past so you can experience the joy of the future. Without forgiveness, you can never heal. You can't afford not to forgive. You don't want to deal with the long-term consequences of bitterness. You don't need the additional weight that comes from harbored resentment. Holding on to those feelings isn't worth it. Withholding forgiveness doesn't punish the offender, it only punishes you.

The long-term effects of bitterness and anger (and the inner stress that those powerful emotions create) have been well-documented in recent years. They produce hormones which contribute to a breakdown in the immune system and can even have connections to heart disease.[2] Withholding forgiveness doesn't stop at robbing you of relationships or emotional well-being. It steals your life from you. Bitterness, resentment, and anger erase precious seconds which make up minutes, hours, days, and even years that disappear from your life before you've had a chance to experience them. Can anything be worth that kind of price? Failing to forgive robs and kills.

FORGIVING ALLOWS YOU TO RECEIVE FORGIVENESS

Those who have difficulty forgiving others often harbor another common trait. When you find it difficult to forgive, you will also find it difficult to receive forgiveness. Forgiving yourself when you have hurt someone can be equally as difficult as forgiving someone who has hurt you. Sometimes it can be even more painful. Perhaps that's why Jesus said what He did. In teaching His followers how to pray, He cautioned that if we are holding a grudge against someone, we should take the initiative to right that damaged relationship. Only then, He said, could we pray with effectiveness and find an open ear from God. God's forgiveness is available to those who themselves show a forgiving spirit. Why? Because we cannot really experience God's forgiveness until we understand the pain and joy of forgiveness through our own personal experience. You will be hurt, and you will hurt someone you care about. Learn to forgive so that you can know the joy and freedom of being forgiven.

FORGIVENESS ALLOWS YOU TO REBUILD RELATIONSHIPS

Most broken relationships are not beyond repair. The typical relationship where we need to show forgiveness can be repaired rather easily when egos are put aside, time is taken to straighten out the facts, and there is a willingness to move on and rebuild. Far from ruining a relationship, an experience of mutual forgiveness can create a depth of friendship that might never be experienced otherwise. Those who have never reclaimed and restored a broken relationship are probably not experiencing relationships at the most rewarding level.

On October 13, 1972, a plane filled with a young rugby team from Uruguay, some family, and the flight crew crashed at 11,500 feet, in the treacherous Andes Mountains. Thirty-three of the forty-five on board survived the initial crash. Only sixteen survived the seventy-two days on the mountain and lived to tell their story. The story of their survival is as incredible as it is inspiring. They slept on top of each other to survive the cold. They cried together on hearing the radio news that the search had been called off. They lived on the flesh of their dead friends' bodies. Two of them, Roberto Carnessi and Nando Perrado, hiked forty miles in ten days to successfully get help and save the others. Their story is filled with episodes of sharp disagreement, painful hurts, and competitive desires. Having been forced by their situation to work through these problems, the bond that those surviving men have with each other is probably as strong as any has ever been. They stay in close contact with each other and regularly meet to reminisce about how they survived "the mountain."

There is something special and binding that we experience through facing struggle and pain together. Restored relationships often have a depth of love which is beyond compare. Don't lose the opportunity to experience that yourself. Make forgiveness a natural part of your life and relationships. Initiate a spirit of forgiveness and humility among those you know. When you do, you will be on the road toward building a network of beneficial relationships which will lead you to discover real happiness and real success.

PART TWO

THE CRUTCH OF
LAZINESS

Mastering Your Life

PART TWO

"The average person puts only 25 percent
of his energy and ability into his work.
The world takes off its hat to those who put more than
50 percent of their capacity, and stands on its head for
those few and far between souls who devote 100 percent."[1]
ANDREW CARNEGIE

Who among us has not wondered about what could have been? Unlike James Bartley, our survivor from the sperm whale's stomach, Caesar Beltram of Lyons, France, perhaps holds the dubious honor as the unluckiest person who has ever pumped blood through his arteries. The poor guy was struck by lightning an amazing and unprecedented five times during his lifetime! If you can believe it, none of those strikes killed him. Instead he died of pneumonia.

If he has been outdone, it may be by a friend of Paul Harvey's named Patricia Christy. Paul reports that after Hurricane Andrew devastated southern Florida, Patricia vowed that she was going to get out of that state. She was determined to leave on the first plane and have herself a restful vacation. A short time later Paul Harvey's voice trumpeted these words, "I have just heard from Patricia Christy. She was standing in line for fresh water on the Hawaiian island of Kauai, having just gone through Hurricane Aniki!"

You could say that luck is a major player in the game of life. Thomas Jefferson said, "I am a great believer in luck, and I find the harder I work the more I have of it." Solomon preceded him with these words, "Lazy people want much but get little, while the diligent are prospering" (Proverbs 13:4 NIV). Do we succeed by luck? Only when that luck is created by lots of hard work. Most of us would like to succeed. Most of us somehow feel a sense of entitlement to success. You have seen that success is not a matter of money, fame, or power. Success comes through the diligence of becoming all that God wants us to be.

During that process, you sometimes stumble over the crutch of laziness. How do you keep from failing to measure up to what you coulda', woulda', shoulda' been? How do you find internal motivation to keep up the fight? How do you tackle life rather than allowing life to handle you? You throw away the crutch called laziness. You can get a new grip on life when you realize the importance of three integral elements which you must master. One, the lasting defeat of the problem of procrastination as a habit and hindrance. Two, learning the life process of evaluating and eliminating the useless and damaging from your life. And three, making discipline an essential and effective part of your character.

CHAPTER

4

DEFEATING
PROCRASTINATION

*"Putting off an easy thing makes it hard,
and putting off a hard one makes it impossible."*[1]
GEORGE H. LORIMER

IF YOU'VE EVER STRUGGLED
with the dreaded adversary called procrastination, you can rest
assured that you've had some famous company. Throughout
history people have struggled with how to motivate themselves to
action. It is said that the French novelist Victor Hugo ordered his
servants to confiscate his clothes and not return them until his
scheduled writing time was completed. Feeling the temptation to
neglect his scholarly work, Demosthenes reportedly shaved one
side of his head so that he would be ashamed to be seen in public.

We've even heard of a chartered Procrastinator's Club whose members live by the credo, "If you put off enough things until later, you'll discover that most of them didn't need to be done in the first place."[3] This said by the group famous for their fun and festive annual Christmas party held religiously each June. If you are like most, you sometimes suffer from the desire to put off until tomorrow what could be done today. In fact, Dr. William Knaus, in a *U.S. News & World Report* article, documents that as many as ninety percent of us suffer from procrastination.[4]

THE PRICE OF PROCRASTINATION

It is certainly not unnatural to procrastinate concerning taking out the trash and cleaning the house. But Dr. Knaus suggests that, while it is common and harmless to procrastinate on those unpleasant tasks you don't enjoy, the problem is that your procrastination tends to become a natural part of your regular behavior. It can easily become a lifestyle pattern which leads you to mediocrity in numerous areas of your life. You may be able to live with putting off those mundane household chores, but can you live with procrastination that costs you significant amounts of time, money, personal fulfillment, and success? To procrastinate in ways that cause us to fail to reach our goals or fail to realize our potential should certainly be unacceptable to us all. The truth is that there is a heavy price that comes with the habit of procrastination.

LOST OPPORTUNITIES

Nothing can be sadder than looking back on life and saying, If only . . . I wish I had . . . Why did I wait so long to . . . I can't believe I didn't . . . . We love John Greenleaf Whittier's statement, "For of all sad words of tongue or pen, the saddest are these: 'It might have been!'"⁵ Perhaps the heaviest price of procrastination comes in the form of lost opportunities. We have seen scores of people blow clear opportunities to better their lives, save their families, turn to God, or improve their financial situations. While you are busy postponing, life is busy passing you by. Sometimes opportunity doesn't knock twice. You have to be ready to jump when opportunity calls.

PROBLEMS MULTIPLIED

Solomon, the wisest man who ever lived, put it bluntly when he said, "A lazy fellow has trouble all through life" (Proverbs 15:19). Procrastination has an incredible way of turning a simple problem into a crisis and a routine situation into a disaster. Craig remembers one day passing an eighteen-wheeler in his Jeep Cherokee. A pebble the size of a pea flew off of that flatbed trailer and hit his windshield. When he saw the tiny crack on the extreme passenger side edge of the windshield, he thought, "I better get that fixed before it spreads." Twelve months later he was being forced to peer around a crack that had grown 46 inches and now spanned from one edge to the other. Now he was thinking, "I better get that fixed before my windshield falls into my lap." The real sting came when his procrastination turned a $10 repair job into a $150 new windshield. Procrastination multiplies our problems. George H. Lorimer once said, "Putting off an easy thing makes it hard, and putting off a hard one makes it impossible." Who knows how many of our difficulties are of our own doing? Samuel Smiles has said, "It will generally be found that men who are constantly lamenting their ill luck are only reaping the consequences of their own neglect, mismanagement, and improvidence." In every area procrastination multiplies our difficulties.

In fact, it was Benjamin Franklin who coined the phrase, "Never leave till tomorrow that which you can do today." The problem with procrastination is that it hurts lots of people, not simply those who are doing the procrastinating. It leaves a trail of half-done, uncompleted projects that contribute to wasted time and energy of those who clean up the messes. Sometimes you put things off out of fear. Fear of the dentist. Fear of that career change. Fear of that sales call. Sometimes you procrastinate as a way of exerting control over a situation or person. You may not be able to erase your bills, but you can put them off. You may not have the final say with your boss, but you can drag your feet. You can even procrastinate by busying yourself in all the wrong activities. The world is full of busybuts (people busy . . . but doing the wrong things). It is, unfortunately, all too easy to find yourself in the unsavory position of the grasshopper in Aesop's fable, "The Grasshopper and the Ant."

Presently up came a grasshopper and begged the ants to spare her a few grains, "For," she said, "I am simply starving." The ants stopped work for a moment, though this was against their principles. "May we ask," said they, "what were you were doing with yourself all last summer? Why didn't you collect a store of food for the winter?" "The fact is," replied the grasshopper, "I was so busy singing that I hadn't the time."

The bottom line is that procrastinating hurts you personally. It keeps you from reaching your goals. It contributes to not feeling good about yourself. Even worse, it hurts those around you. Though you may realize that putting things off will only lead to additional problems, that is no guarantee that it will motivate you to stop procrastinating. Because it is such an ingrained behavior, procrastination certainly is a difficult cycle to break. So what is the answer?

WINNING OVER PROCRASTINATION

Isn't it amazing how we try to con ourselves and rationalize our own self-defeating behavior? Call it what you like—deferring, postponing, suspending, putting on the back burner, keeping in a holding pattern, calling a time-out. Procrastination is procrastination by any name, and it is likely that you don't need us or anyone else to prove that point to you. What you want is someone to give you some practical steps to help you master the dreaded nemesis. The question remains, how do you win over procrastination? We live by the adage that, "Anyone can show me my problem, but I'll love the one who shows me how to overcome it."

THE IMPORTANCE OF ATTITUDE

We have found that the key to conquering the habit of procrastination and postponing is the development of the right attitude. Widely read author Chuck Swindoll sums up the importance of attitude about as well as we've seen it done. "The longer I live, the more I realize the impact of attitude on life." Chuck goes on to say, "Attitude, to me, is more important than facts. It is more important than the past, than education, than money, than circumstances, than failures, than successes, than what other people think or say or do. It is more important than appearance, giftedness, or skill." There is a great deal in life that is beyond our control. You can't change the past. You have only a limited impact on the future. You have little or no say in the way some people will act. An infinite number of circumstances are outside of our power, but one thing you can control is your attitude. No one can affect your attitude unless you give them permission. Swindoll later says, "I am convinced that life is ten percent what happens to me and ninety percent how I react to it." Of the many things that attitude affects, procrastination is one of the most significant. Develop the right attitude and beat procrastination.

A DECISIVE ATTITUDE

Someone once said that the opposite of procrastination is decision. In other words, to procrastinate is to postpone making a decision. If you think about when you procrastinate and what you procrastinate about, you will discover exactly how true that is. You put off paying the bills because you never really decide when you are going to do it. You just leave it out there as something you need to do. You don't really want to do it, so it keeps getting pushed down the list. Soon they are past due. You don't clean the garage because it is just something that you need to do. You know it should be done, but it's not something you are looking forward to beginning. The result—it doesn't get done. There really is a simple way to solve this situation. Decide to do it. Schedule it, and do it on schedule. Forget the I need to's, the I want to's, the I plan to's, the I hope I can's. Decide.

Procrastination is mentally exhausting. It is a heavy weight which is bearing down on you constantly. To make a decision and follow through with it is exhilarating. A quality decision is specific (date and time). A quality decision is concrete (it can hold up under accountability.) It is impossible for procrastination and decision to live in the same household. To understand that can be revolutionary and transformational. Soon your decisive attitude will reap benefits of more time for yourself, more accomplishment, a better feeling about yourself, and a break-up of the habit of procrastination.

A NO-EXCUSE ATTITUDE

Have you ever noticed how other people have excuses, and we have reasons? We almost always have good reasons why we have put something off. Benjamin Franklin spoke frankly when he said, "The people who are good at making excuses are rarely good at anything else." King Solomon said it as well in the Proverbs, "A lazy man is full of excuses. 'I can't go to work!' He says, 'If I go outside I might meet a lion in the street and be killed!" We can laugh all right at such an absurd excuse, but if we are honest we will often find that our excuses are no better. We ran across these true statements (excuses) taken from submitted insurance forms:

"Going home from work I drove into the wrong house and collided with a tree I don't have."

"The guy was all over the road, I had to swerve a number of times before I hit him . . . ."

"As I pulled away from the side of the road, I glanced at my mother-in-law and headed over the embankment."

"In my attempt to kill a fly I ran into a telephone pole."

"I was on my way to the doctor with rear end trouble when my universal joints gave way, causing me to have an accident."

"I had been driving my car for forty years when I fell asleep at the wheel and had an accident."

"The telephone pole was approaching fast. I attempted to swerve off its path when it struck my front end."

Our favorite...

"The pedestrian had no idea which way to go, so I ran over him."

What's your excuse? What is it in your life that you know you need to change, but you've been putting it off? What is there that you know you need to do, but you haven't? To win over procrastination you must decide that excuses are no longer a valid part of your way of thinking. Attitude is something no one can have for you. No amount of money can buy an attitude. No amount of influence can peddle one. You are the only one that can produce your attitude. To conquer procrastination you must develop the attitude that says "I will make no more excuses. I'll just do it. If I don't do it as well as I hoped, I will do it better next time. I decide for myself that I am responsible for my actions. I and only I am responsible for my failures. In the same way, I and only I can be responsible for my successes. When it comes to beating procrastination, I will succeed without excuse."

A PASSIONATE ATTITUDE

Of all the things that will help you break the cycle of procrastination, possibly the most significant is developing a life passion. When you put off changes and find it difficult to get motivated to reach your potential, it is often because a sense of life apathy has set in. Dr. Charles Garfield, in his book *Peak Performers*, studied people who have achieved significant, even phenomenal success. There he makes a rather stunning statement when he writes, "Peak performers are people who really understand that the best use of a life is committed action to a mission that they care deeply about." That really is a staggering assertion. We might expect that these peak performers have certain similarities in education, IQ, temperament, personality, family background, or social status. We might anticipate that their success is related to experience, talent, looks, good fortune, or inside connections. In actuality the driving force behind significant success is the belief that what you are doing has real significance. That is passion. Do you have a belief, even a conviction that what you are doing matters? James Barrie says, "Nothing is work unless you would rather be doing something else." It is that kind of spirit that has led to some of the most phenomenal success stories we have known.

One of the more famous stories and spectacular accomplishments is the dramatic pulling together of the NASA team to put the first man on the moon. When President John F. Kennedy announced in the early 1960s that Americans would be the first to put a man on the moon, it was quite literally an impossible task. There was no technology available that would allow us to do that. It was simply a bold and dramatic statement of vision. What followed was a testimony to the power of the human spirit to rally around a cause, to motivate themselves to accomplish what seemed to be an impossible task. Their passion for reaching the visionary goal proclaimed by Kennedy made procrastination an extinct concept. Those on the NASA team were driven to change the world, and "what if" and "but" had no place in their vocabulary.

Yet you might say, "Great for them! But I don't have a glamorous job with world-changing implications!" All the more reason for you to find a passion for which you can live. There is a great deal of truth in the old story about the two men who met at the subway station. One man asked the other, "What line of work are you in?" The man responded, "I'm a Christian." "No, I mean what is your job?" Again the reply, "I am a Christian." After a few moments of puzzled silence he went on, "But I am a plumber to pay the bills." That is what you call passion. This person doesn't have to search for external motivation because he has a passion for living which brings joy and purpose and makes procrastination an uninvited guest at a private party. There is no reason to put things off because you know where you are going and you can always see the bigger picture. It is that kind of spirit that produces peak performance. We will have a great deal more to say on this point later, especially as we discuss the development of your vision. For now you might ask yourself this question, "How passionate is my attitude for life?" It may have more impact than you imagine.

We ran across an interview of a well-known actress describing how her friends used to try to talk her out of being an actress. She lit up as she said, "If someone doesn't have a passion—whether it's playing the guitar or manipulating the stock market—you can't explain it to them, because it's got nothing to do with practicality." To overcome procrastination, or even more significantly, to move toward realizing your personal potential, is to find a niche which allows you to know that you are contributing something to this big, impersonal world. Maybe it's the attitude that, "I'm not just a teacher; I'm the molder of young minds and spirits that will one day be doctors, lawyers, pastors, CEOs, and presidents." Maybe it's, "I'm not just a mother raising kids; I'm the primary influencer of my kids concerning God, values, love, and relationships in life." For Jim, it's helping people grow in character and confidence as they find financial freedom. For Craig, it's helping people discover the reality and the relevance of a vital relationship with God. It's not really what you do that matters, but the spirit and the attitude with which you do it. If you can't find that passion in what you're doing now, do something else, but by all means find your passion. You may find it to be a help in a variety of areas, not the least of which is procrastination.

A "NOW/NOW" ATTITUDE

There is a dangerous way of thinking prevalent among many today. It is dangerous because it is self-deceiving. Because of its deception, many don't even recognize it as procrastination, and this may lend to its being the worst kind of procrastinating. We call it the "when/then" principle. The principle goes something like this: "When I get ____, then I will ____." Fill in the blanks with anything you like. When I get a million dollars, then I will be happy. When I have more time, then I will start going to church. When it starts affecting my job, then I'll quit drinking. When my wife begins treating me well, then I will treat her well. When I ____, then I'll ____. On and on we could go.

We're not describing the sometimes useful tool of rewarding ourselves for achieving. The reward method of motivation says, "When I accomplish my quota of sales calls this week, then I will reward myself with dinner out Friday evening." That type of internal motivation can be helpful in causing you to stay diligent toward reaching your goals. If dangling these types of rewards can prompt you to accomplish more, then by all means do it. But we are describing a much more sinister self-deception, which is the "when/then" principle. The "when/then" principle is not about rewards; it is about character.

For instance, Craig often has to teach people the principle of tithing ten percent of our income to God. That is a concept that many find difficult to swallow. People often use the "when/then" principle like this: "I don't make enough money to tithe right now. When I make more money, then I will tithe." Unfortunately we have seldom found that to work. In fact, if you can't give ten dollars on a hundred, we can nearly guarantee you will never give

$100,000 on a million! You see, tithing is not a question of money, it's a question of character. So is being happy, treating others well, going to church, spending time with your kids—you get the point. If you don't do those things now, it's unlikely that you will do them when circumstances change. Why? Because we're talking about character. We're talking about values.

Procrastination can be a most difficult pattern to break, especially when it deals with a fundamental need for character change. Quit saying "when/then", and begin developing your "now/now" attitude. Jesus said that he who is faithful in little will be given much. That is the "now/now" principle. Don't make your happiness, your good will, your habits, your integrity, or anything else conditional. Make your happiness, your good will, your habits, your integrity, or anything else absolute. Do it now because it is right. Do it now because it is you. Do it now because it's your character. That will beat procrastination at its roots.

If you really crave breaking the cycle of procrastination, it's not complicated, but it's also not easy. Make a conscious decision to do it. Begin today. Hold yourself accountable to someone who knows you well. Then stop making excuses and attack life with a passion.

CHAPTER

5

REFINING THE ART OF EVALUATION AND ELIMINATION

"The trouble with most of us is that we would rather be ruined by praise than saved by criticism."[1]
NORMAN VINCENT PEALE

YOU MAY HAVE HEARD ABOUT the man who was asked the secret of his success. He answered, "I never make the same mistake twice... twice." Unfortunately our lives are often littered with patterns of making the same mistakes over and over... and over. Often successful lives and careers are undercut by blatant and unmanaged personal weaknesses. The successful businessman moves from one broken marriage to a second broken marriage because he doesn't see what has caused the first failed relationship. An inability to communicate on an intimate level was mistaken for "love grown cold." The second could have been saved from what killed the first... if only. The loving mother can't understand why her child shows such little self-restraint. What she attributes to having "a strong-willed child" is really a result of her own lack of consistency in setting behavioral limits for her son. Both mother and child could have been more happy and secure... if only. Cycles of self-defeating habits are quite often our downfall. It is all too easy to wear blinders when it comes to looking honestly at ourselves. Have you ever noticed how easy it is to spot the faults of others, and yet how difficult it is to master your own shortcomings and weaknesses? It's interesting that this was the message of Jesus in His classic and most extensive teaching in the Bible.

> *Why do you notice the little piece of dust that is in your brother's eye, but you don't notice the big piece of wood that is in your own eye? Why do you say to your brother, "Let me take that little piece of dust out of your eye?" Look at yourself first! You still have that big piece of wood in your own eye.*
>
> MATTHEW 7:3-4

In the study of world history we find a puzzling phenomenon. The mistakes of the past are normally repeated again in the future. On a personal level many of us all too often repeat the mistakes of the past as well. To be able to learn from your mistakes as well as from those of others is a valuable life lesson.

THE TANGIBLE IMPACT OF SELF-DEFEATING BEHAVIOR

Cycles of weakness and failure will keep you from achieving your goals. John won't reach his company-set goal of $10,000 in sales this month because his lack of discipline has prevented him from making enough calls. Peter wants to improve his marriage, but he missed an opportunity to encourage his wife because of his lack of empathy and his preoccupation with his own agenda. Your weaknesses have direct and noticeable results in your life. Blindness to your own character flaws inevitably will affect your career progress, your family happiness, your physical fitness, your bank account balances, and right down the line we could go. Often we find a domino effect where each area of life is impacted, all stemming from some unresolved personal flaw.

How about one illustration. Joe has an unresolved character flaw—he struggles with moodiness. The results are clear. His co-workers are wary of him because they are never sure how he will respond in a crisis. This is noticed by his bosses, and he is passed over for promotion. Angry and insecure about that, he brings his frustration home to his relationship with his wife. His teenage daughter is getting further alienated from him because of his volatile temper. At every stage the results are measurable and real. With some personal evaluation and appropriate action the results could be quite different.

THE MENTAL IMPACT OF SELF-DEFEATING BEHAVIOR

But a more subtle and significant price of your unmanaged faults also comes due. What your unrecognized and unresolved weaknesses do is gradually kill your motivation to achieve. Eventually your spirit, enthusiasm, and motivation will suffer. Your psyche can handle only so much until you mentally throw in the towel, determined not to suffer another humiliating failure again. God only knows how many men and women through history were filled with unused potential. Potential that was unused because their will to achieve had been beaten down by unresolved personal character and personality defects. It is difficult to maintain the motivation to achieve when you encounter defeat piled up on defeat. Once you reach the quitting stage, it is difficult to renew the motivation to achieve. We have witnessed people who no longer believe they can achieve. Not only are these situations incredibly tragic, they are completely unnecessary! Too many times it is because of some changeable personal flaws which have never been changed. Over time the scars from personal failure can become permanent. It doesn't have to be that way for you.

HOW TO WIN OVER SELF-DEFEATING BEHAVIOR

A priceless quality in staying motivated for achievement is mastery of the skill of evaluating and eliminating. Anyone who strives to reach his best is compelled to ask himself the hard questions. "What are my weaknesses?" "Where can I improve?" "What are my character flaws?" "Where could I have improved in my relationships today?" To be successful does not mean that you have the innate ability to avoid mistakes; it means that you have learned to grow from your mistakes through the principles of evaluation and elimination. Some of the most successful people in history are also prime examples of people who simply learned from their mistakes.

We looked at evaluating mistakes in the decision-making process. Now we're getting personal. How do you learn from your personal mistakes? You evaluate why you failed, and you eliminate the cause. In advertising lingo, "It's that simple! Period." There is nothing quite as scary as making the decision to take an honest look at yourself. The thought of such self-evaluation is about as appealing as listening to yourself on audio tape, or worse yet, watching yourself on video tape. Few people like the prospect of making self-scrutiny and self-inspection a regular part of their routine. Yet it is valuable for the person serious about being his personal best.

EVALUATION

Few would argue that it is quality in business that assures long-term success. One businessman, famous for his hotels and business parks, is quoted as saying, "I've never been satisfied with anything we've ever built. I've felt that dissatisfaction is the basis of progress. When we become satisfied in business we become obsolete."[2] It is that kind of passion for quality that drove Ray Kroc, the founder of McDonald's, to build his empire around quality. So driven was Kroc that he once said, "If I had a brick for every time I repeated the phrase Q.S.C.& V (Quality, Service, Cleanliness, and Value), I think I'd probably be able to bridge the Atlantic Ocean with them."[3] The Niemann-Marcus Department Store has long been known for prestige and quality. Stanley Marcus tells of the time that Tennessean Jack Massey was trying to get married in Texas when the presiding judge wanted to see some identification. The bride was only able to produce a Niemann-Marcus credit card, to which the judge responded, "Well, if your credit is good with them, it's good with me."[4] Such a reputation for excellence does not come by chance. The founder of Niemann-Marcus was always asking how the merchandise offered to customers could be improved. To eliminate flaws, the company established an inspection department in which every article of apparel could be tried on a model form and checked for fit and defects. Only then could it be offered to customers.

The question we should ask of ourselves is this. Isn't our personal life worthy of the same standard of excellence and expectations as hamburgers and business suits? You may think that such evaluation is fine for business, but it really doesn't matter for yourself. After all, you just want to be happy, you're not driven for perfection. We couldn't disagree more! We're not talking about perfection. We're talking about objectively evaluating those things in life that are weights around your ankles and constantly holding you back from achievement and personal happiness. As it does for business, the ability to objectively and honestly evaluate yourself will certainly show tremendous rewards in the quality of your life. Someone has said, "The person afraid of self-examination can be certain that things need examining." The philosopher Socrates said it in even stronger terms, "The unexamined life isn't worth living." It would certainly seem clear that consistent and conscientious self-evaluation is not an option but a requirement for the person determined to rise above complacency and mediocrity and become the best that he can be.

Certainly one of the most successful lives ever lived was that of the Apostle Paul, writer of nearly half of the Bible's New Testament. He was an entrepreneur of renown. Paul almost single-handedly was responsible for starting dozens of influential new Christian churches throughout the Middle East and Europe. He fought against false teachings which threatened the viability of the early church's existence. He put into writing much of Christian theology. He was a brilliant thinker and a tireless worker. He worked the graveyard shift to support himself in the often thankless work of spreading the Christian faith. He endured shipwrecks, torture, numerous extended jail terms, snake bites, physical exhaustion, an unknown ailment he called a "thorn in the flesh," and ultimately the death of a martyr. His legacy—millions of Christians who owe their life view as well as their happiness to this tireless man of conviction. What do we learn from this great man's life story? One major lesson is very evident.

PERSONAL TRANSPARENCY

Paul was not afraid for others to see who he really was. He was open and honest about his faults and weaknesses. He was brutally candid about his inner struggles. Anyone who has read the seventh chapter of Paul's letter to the Romans can immediately identify with the tumultuous personal struggles with which he wrestled. In that chapter Paul describes how he desperately wanted to do the right thing. Yet, somehow, no matter how hard he tried, he often couldn't follow through. Likewise, more than anything he wanted to avoid doing the wrong things, but too often he found himself unable to avoid those things he most hated. No honest person could say that he hasn't experienced the pull of those same emotions. It was that kind of sincere personal transparency that characterized Paul. He knew that God loved and accepted him. As a result, he was able to openly share with others who he really was and the personal issues with which he dealt. His hope was that his honesty would help others in their struggles.

Paul's intense honesty in communication is evidence of his willingness to look at himself. Few people have what some counselors call "an observing self." An observing self is the ability to objectively look at how others are viewing you, what your attitude is communicating, how you are hurting people, whether your activities are really effective. Cultivating your ability to objectively observe and evaluate yourself is the key to emotional health and effective personal growth. For most of us, looking in-depth at who we are is not something we either practice or relish the thought of doing. Jim has a colleague who has often impressed him with his desire to grow. On a regular basis he would ask the simple question, "Jim, how can I be better?" That question must be asked by those who grow. There is no other way to discover the value or the joy of personal improvement. If you ever hope to advance from where you are today, personal transparency is the only road out of town.

Personal potential is not something you attain. It is something you strive towards. You will never reach a level where you can quit. Don't let that be a discouragement for you. While you will never arrive at your destination, you will reach a level where you will recognize that you have made significant progress and have improved your quality of life. That is the motivation that keeps you going. Things can be better tomorrow if you honestly and objectively evaluate today.

Are you willing to give yourself a personal inventory? The exciting part about identifying your personal character flaws is that your weaknesses have the potential to become your greatest strengths. We will talk more about this in a moment.

Sit down today and honestly confront your character, your values and how you apply them, your relationships and how you operate in them. You may be surprised at what you discover. It could be the key to moving beyond where you are today. Make honest self-evaluation a part of your daily routine. Make a habit of asking yourself if you are a part of the problem or a part of the solution. "How could I have used my time more wisely today? Did I show compassion to that person I spoke with this morning? How did my character flaw of anger hurt me today?" Consistent practice of the principle of evaluation will keep you from confronting the major disasters which result from neglecting your personal lives.

ELIMINATION

Eliminating the worthless is one of the most natural processes in the world. Every day we breath in air, keeping the life-giving oxygen while eliminating the carbon dioxide. Our bodies take nutrients from the food we eat and eliminate what is not productive. That is all a part of living, and our emotional lives should function on the same principle. Upon evaluating your life, you should keep the good and eliminate the bad. You should retain the positive and oust the negative. You should welcome the worthwhile and evict the worthless. That is healthy living. To allow unproductive thoughts, negative attitudes, hurtful behaviors, and harmful habits to clutter your life benefits no one. In all of that you are allowing the mistakes of your past to control your present and future. All of that could be stopped by practicing the habit of elimination.

Typically the majority of people fall into one of two traps. Many people are keenly aware of their own faults. They beat themselves up constantly because of them. But this becomes a life habit in and of itself. They don't move forward by letting go of past. Instead, they are controlled by it. They relive those past failures over and over in their minds. They are never able to move on with freedom and new insight. Let's take our friend Phlegmatic

Phil as an example. Phil was always seen as shy growing up. Often he was overlooked in the classroom and on the playground. It seemed that the attention he wanted from his family and friends was always reserved for someone else. Phil found it difficult to build relationships, and more and more he withdrew into his self-made, protective shell. Though he didn't understand at the time, Phil began to get attention by messing up in school. He found an accepting group of friends and moved through life without venturing far from that which was comfortable. This behavior became habit, and Phil became an underachiever. His abilities and potential were vast, but he was unwilling to invest in developing them for fear of failure. Phil could not recognize and cultivate his strengths because he was too keenly aware of the presence of his weaknesses. The past had paralyzed him.

Many others, though, find the opposite characteristics true for them. They move through life with freedom, but are unwilling or unable to look at their past mistakes. They never look at themselves objectively, rarely learn from mistakes, and never make progress. They are not paralyzed by past failures, but because they don't learn from the past, the past controls them nonetheless. Let's look at Sparky Sam. Sam grew up as the life of the party. He made people laugh with ease and soon learned to rely on the charming aspects of his personality to get him through life. He was always picked to be a leader, was always looked up to by his peers for approval, was voted most popular, and was deemed most likely to succeed. But there was one problem. Because he had ridden the strengths of his wonderful personality, he had failed to deal with the more weighty and substantial matters of long-term success. He had glaring flaws related to dependability, perseverance, and discipline. His abundant potential was never realized and his significant gifts remained under-utilized. How did this happen? Sam had failed to look objectively at his life and make necessary course corrections in matters of character. Both of the extremes of Phlegmatic Phil and Sparky Sam are disastrous. You may fall somewhere in the middle. Wherever you fall, it is essential that you develop the ability to learn from the past, without dwelling on it. It is imperative that you learn and practice the habit of elimination.

However you are able to do it, it must be done. To be successful you must be able to evaluate yourself and let go of the negative. While that is easy to say, letting go of the negative is not so easy to accomplish. Many of your habits may be deeply embedded into your character. Many of your past hurts may make it difficult to find freedom. We frequently hear this question asked in a variety of ways, "Why is life so hard?" It is precisely here that you can discover one of the most rewarding and fulfilling benefits of being a Christian. You learn that hardship and trial are always for the purpose of developing your character. The Bible uses the illustration of the refiner's fire. The goldsmith heaps his mounds of raw gold together and begins the refining process. He fires the gold with a white-hot flame until the gold melts into a boiling liquid. As the gold cools and hardens, a substance rises to the top, which the goldsmith calls dross. The dross is all the impurities within the gold that steal its value and make it just another rock. This refining process is continued until nothing remains except the brilliant and valuable gold. It is a process similar to this in which you find the path to developing your character and achieving your potential. It is sometimes painful, but the brilliant and valuable results are always worth it.

In your relationship with God you should know that God

promises to help you with any challenge that you may encounter. That includes finding mastery over character flaws. He created you, and He can certainly help you deal with those damaging qualities which are threatening to shipwreck you. More than that, you can have freedom of conscience for all of those times you have hurt others, hurt God, and hurt yourself. God willingly offers His forgiveness to those who commit their lives to following Him. God's pattern for dealing with past failures is amazingly simple. Confess your failure. Ask for His power to overcome them. He will empower you to a victorious life through the habits of evaluation and elimination.

6

IMPROVING YOUR DISCIPLINE

*"Would you live with ease, do what you ought
and not what you please."*[1]
BENJAMIN FRANKLIN

WHAT MAKES SOME PEOPLE
successful at nearly everything they do while others never seem to
measure up? Why do some seem to find accomplishment easy, and
others fight and struggle for everything they get? If someone could
bottle the answer to those questions, they would stand to make
quite a lot of money. But bottled formulas are not the answer.
Searching the bookstores for a four-step formula for success is not
a realistic solution either. The secret only comes through realizing
your full potential, and one of the most prominent ingredients in

that is the character quality of discipline. If you are like most people, discipline is not one of those things that comes naturally and without significant effort. As John Burroughs once said, "For anything worth having one must pay the price; and the price is always work, patience, love, self-sacrifice." Developing discipline is hard work. It is dirty work. Discipline is certainly one of those traits for which you must pay a price, yet it is an indispensable characteristic for you to develop as you work towards becoming your very best. There is no substitute for discipline.

The New York City executive search firm of C. Stewart Baeder Associates conducted a survey of its clients, asking what qualities they most looked for in their top executives. The results were surprising. They didn't look first for an MBA, for a certain personality type, or even for a lengthy list of high-profile experience. The number one, most desired quality was self-discipline (89%), followed by general administrative skills (82%), and an aptitude for human relations (70%). Why do we find that surprising? Because we typically believe, subconsciously at least, that successful people are somehow more fortunate, more naturally gifted, or simply better connected than we are. Is success simply a matter of being at the right place at the right time? We don't think so. In our experience, when we look at people who have achieved in many areas of life, we have found that one common denominator is the character trait of discipline.

On the contrary, when you look closely at the lives of those who have fallen short of their potential, you often find a common root—a nagging lack of self-discipline. Solomon in all his wisdom saw the pervasiveness of a lack of discipline and found an example in the most unlikely of places:

Take a lesson from the ants, you lazy fellow. Learn from their ways and be wise! For though they have no king to make them work, yet they labor hard all summer, gathering food for the winter.

PROVERBS 6:6-8 (LB)

Few people need to be convinced of their need to develop more self-discipline. Those who lack it usually know it better than anyone. Unfortunately, discipline seems to be something that few people are born with. Some are definitely blessed with a personality that makes the development of discipline easier. But none are born disciplined. Discipline is developed. If it's one of your Achilles' heels, be encouraged that you are not alone. Be more encouraged that an understanding and practice of the proper principles can put you on the path to a more disciplined lifestyle.

THE LANGUAGE OF DISCIPLINE

There's a certain language that disciplined people understand and use in everyday living. For the person of discipline, speaking this language through their lifestyle is as simple and comfortable as a well-worn living room recliner. The language really represents a way of living that allows them to harness the incredible power that discipline can bring. This language of discipline is illustrated by three adages. Let's examine them one at a time.

ADAGE #1

"I will pay now so I can enjoy later."

The nature of discipline is nothing new. The concepts have been around for ages, and many people have taught them. Craig remembers sitting in his ninth-grade civics course. Among the topics studied was a principle his teacher called delayed gratification. "Delayed gratification," he said, "is enduring the initial sacrifice so I can fully enjoy its benefits later." It is in this principle that we find the essence of discipline. Simply put, discipline is the ability to envision what the reward of your work will be. Discipline understands that you will only find rewards when you are willing to pay the price... first. Discipline says, "I would rather pay now so I can savor the rewards of my labor." Discipline is not about experiencing pain. Discipline is about getting inevitable pain out of the way so that you can fully enjoy the rewards. Lack of discipline almost always brings more pain in the long run. Like the transmission commercial says, "You can pay me now (beep beep) or pay me later." Delayed gratification is the choice to pay now and enjoy the rewards that you know are coming.

Since the beginning of the American society, saving money was a highly valued practice. People not only understood, but they practiced delayed gratification. Somehow that once prized value has faded in significance today. Our value sometimes seems to be more in line with "let's have it all... now!" rather than "let's earn it so we can enjoy it!" Plastic credit cards have made it easy to enjoy material possessions now and pay for them later. This instant gratification mentality is now showing up in other areas of our lives, and suddenly we have become a generation of people who do not know how to consistently apply delayed gratification to our finances, our relationships, our careers, our spiritual development, or much of anything else.

The concept of delayed gratification is so simple that it is difficult to discuss at length. Delaying gratification increases the rewards you receive. It is a concept simple to grasp, but much more difficult to apply. It is more than a concept to understand, it is a conviction to live by. There is really little argument that delayed gratification is critical. However, you will not practice delayed gratification yourself until you become personally convinced of its rewards for you. When you do, it will become a valuable part of your character and your road toward success.

Case in point: Relationships are tough to build and maintain. To develop a fulfilling marriage takes a great deal of time, attention, and maybe even sleepless nights. Bill and Lynn Hybels in their book *Fit to Be Tied* describe the struggles that they shared in their sometimes turbulent marriage. There were long, silent car rides and countless misunderstandings. Learning to openly and effectively communicate with each other, share common experiences, wrestle with vast differences in personality and style, and a host of other issues all took years and included many sleepless nights. Both share openly in their book about the changes they have made and the struggles of staying married against the odds. Both also share that the pain and struggle are well worth it in the end. There is no other way to experience true intimacy in marriage. All of us long for a relationship of depth which will give us fulfillment and joy. Sometimes realizing that type of relationship takes years, and often it is just over the horizon when people throw in the towel. When you practice delayed gratification, you understand that the ultimate payoff is worth the initial pain. You work and persevere so you can enjoy the rewards which will one day come. Fill in the blank with anything you like. Whatever it is, the discipline of delayed gratification pays big dividends no matter what the economic times.

Discipline is the ability to remain steadfast and consistent in pursuit of your desired goal. Discipline is a strength of character that is willing to wait for your desired rewards. Real life is not about waiting to win the big sweepstakes. Real life is not waiting for your ship to come in, or to get your big break. There is no easy money, no pain-free relationships, no short cuts to security or happiness. Real life is about finding rewards because you have paid the price. That's real life, and that's discipline.

ADAGE #2

"I will be guided by my decisions, not by my feelings."

The language of discipline says that you won't be ruled by your feelings but by your decisions. We live in a culture that is dominated by emotional living. Vengeance movies teach us to react to life rather than live by principle. We see love as a good feeling rather than a commitment to someone. Advertising convinces us that we must have products that we often don't need. Our principles are blurry, we fall in and out of love, and we buy on impulse. By contrast, emotionalism has very little place when it comes to living a disciplined life. There is nothing wrong with emotions, except when those emotions hinder you from doing the things that you really desire to do, or more importantly those things which are necessary to do. When that happens you are actually ruining your ability to experience the greatest feelings of accomplishment. Discipline is all about deciding in advance what to do and not allowing temporary and unreliable feelings to change your mind.

You will never become disciplined until you make the commitment to be guided by your decisions and principles rather than by your feelings. You will never become disciplined until you make the commitment to be guided by your decisions and principles rather than by your feelings. No, that is not a typo. We say it twice to drive home this important fact. Why is this so critical? It's really simple: feelings change. Emotions can be very deceptive and are not a very trustworthy guide for living life and making decisions. Emotions change as circumstances change, and thus are often in a constant state of flux. Emotions are volatile. When it comes to practicing discipline, feelings are often incompatible. Once you decide what you want to do, you do it based on the decision that you've made. That's discipline. Discipline does not make us less human—it makes us more mature.

Again, our friend James deals with the issue of acting based on decision as he relates it to our faith in God:

> *Do not doubt God. Anyone who doubts is like a wave in the sea. The wind blows the wave up and down. He who doubts is thinking two different things at the same time. He cannot decide about anything he does.*
>
> JAMES 1:6-8 (EB)

Is James saying that we can't have faith in God if we ever have doubts? Of course not. Doubt is a part of the human experience, and even the most committed believer is sometimes plagued by doubt. James is saying that there are two possible decisions to make concerning your relationship with God. Based on the available facts, you either decide not to have faith in God or you decide to place your faith in God. But once you have made the decision to place your faith in God, you should do it without looking back. You must now live your life based on your decision and not on the emotions which might cause you to question or doubt. Discipline is very much the same. When you have made decisions about how to live your life, you must follow through with them.

Let's clear the air with some more concrete examples. John decides that he wants to get in better shape and needs to add a fitness regimen to his weekly schedule. It has become a high priority because of about fifteen excess pounds, blood pressure which is inching higher, and a history of heart disease in his family. He pays for a membership in the local health club and decides he needs to work out three days a week. Here's a common scenario. Monday comes, and John tentatively schedules a work out "after work." The day doesn't go well. There is a conflict with a supervisor, and he has forgotten to prepare for a mid-morning presentation. By mid-afternoon he is tired and decides to postpone his workout until Tuesday. So the week goes, and when Sunday arrives John realizes that he has worked out only once this week. Why? Because he acted by emotion and not by decision.

Instead, by applying advanced decision-making, John will conclude that working out is a priority. Therefore he will go to the gym Monday, Wednesday, and Friday from 5:30 until 6:45. Circumstances have a way of filling in the available time unless we set parameters. With his newly set schedule, and barring any emergency, John will work out Monday, Wednesday, and Friday from 5:30 until 6:45, whether he feels like it or not. It's all too easy to rationalize and say, if I feel like it, if I have time, if I need it . . .

Discipline is not iffy. When it is something you know you should do, you must make the decision and then apply the discipline to do it.

The same principle holds true for every area of your life. Let's say that to reach your goal this month in sales calls, you must make forty calls this week. When you have set the number of sales calls you want to make this week, you must follow through based on your advanced decision. You make eight calls per day. By the end of each day you might not feel like making that extra call. You're tired, cranky and sick of hearing, NO! It doesn't matter. You work from your decisions and not your feelings. If you have wasted time or not prioritized your calls, you are able to follow through at week's end, because you know to trust your decision and not your feelings. In the end your hard work will pay off through increased commissions and a personal feeling of accomplishment. Likewise in your family and spiritual life you must faithfully apply the process of making decisions in advance and living by them. This is the only successful way to be disciplined. It's the only successful way to live.

ADAGE #3

"I will keep busy doing the right things."

Not long ago we saw a movie in which a well-known actor played a successful, high-powered attorney from New York City. He was, of course, brilliant, well-known, and in high demand for his services. In one of the opening scenes he is shown bursting out of his penthouse office, his secretary scuttling behind him as he mercilessly barks out orders. The poor secretary is feverishly scribbling out his instructions as they walk down the corridor. He says something like this: "Cancel my lunch tomorrow. I'm going to work through and move the dinner to next week. Pull the file on Briggs versus Gordon. I need that Martinson deposition on my desk by nine o'clock tomorrow morning. Call my wife and tell her I can't make dinner at 7:30." As he hands his secretary his half-smoked cigarette he walks onto the elevator and concludes, "Tell her to call the Joneses and make it 8:30 instead." The underlying message of this movie scene: important and successful people are busy. Often this is true. People who have achieved success are frequently in great demand for their time, attention, talents, money, and energy. Unfortunately you may apply faulty improper use of logic and erroneously conclude that since successful people are busy, then if you are busy, you are successful! That is not only an obviously wrong conclusion, it can be a dangerous one which can hinder you from reaching true success.

There is no question that in today's hectic and fast-paced lifestyle you may find yourself racing 120 miles an hour to finish everything on your to-do list. But in counseling with hundreds of people, we have concluded that many people today are trying to derive their self-esteem from the busyness of their schedules. It is a mistake to believe that being busy equals being successful. Though a busy schedule is often a by-product of success, it can just as easily be a sign of a cluttered life. In fact, to be busy doing the wrong things is tantamount to doing nothing at all. The Apostle Paul one time chastened a group for this very reason:

> *We hear that some among you are idle. They are not busy, they are busybodies.*
>
> 2 THESSALONIANS 3:11 (NIV)

Like that cluttered closet in your house, it may be that you need to get rid of unneeded and useless activity which is stealing your valuable time and effort.

The right question is not, "Is my schedule full?" The right question is, "What is my schedule full of?" You need to decide whether you want to really be successful or it is good enough to appear successful. To some the appearance of success is all they truly need. If a new car, a nice house, and busy schedule are all you need to feel successful, then you may need to read no further. But if success for you includes a caring home, fulfilling relationships, a life of integrity, and realizing your full potential, then keep on reading, because that's what we mean by success. If you sincerely want to find true success, it will be necessary that you know and apply the rule of prioritization. Prioritization is an essential quality of discipline.

To prioritize your life means that you make advanced decisions on the use of your time based on what is important to you. Your life should revolve around purpose and not pressures. If your life is not driven by your purpose, you will be manipulated by life's pressures and demands. When living by priorities, your schedule will move from a disorganized array of various activities to an arranged assortment of activities which are contributing to reaching your life goals. People who have achieved high levels of success have mastered the ability to prioritize their lives. Sometimes it is the reason they have gotten to where they are; in other cases the time crunch of being successful forced them to prioritize.

However they arrived at it, disciplined, successful people are characterized by a strong understanding of their values. They know what is important to them, and they arrange their lives around it accordingly. Burt Nanus and Warren Bennis, in their book *Leaders,* studied 60 of the nation's top CEOs. These people were described as an exceptionally diverse group at the top of their fields. Their paths to success were varied, and they differed greatly in management style, temperament, perspective, and even dress. Only one surprise cropped up which was worth mentioning. Almost all were married to their first spouses. That is quite a surprising fact when compared to the populace as a whole, which has a much higher rate of divorce.

What is the lesson here? Despite the intense demands on their time, the pressures of responsibility for bottom-line profits, the major day-in/day-out decisions, the supervision of employees, and the myriad of options for company investments, these executives were not overwhelmed to the detriment of their families. These men and women were not simply married to their first spouses; they were still married to their first spouses because they held the institution of marriage in high esteem. It was an important part of their values, and they gave it the necessary time and support. Discipline involves the ability to say no when the pressure to do more does not advance or support your priorities and values. Any activity which vies for your time or attention must pass the test first. Is this something which contributes to your goals for family, career, fitness, relationships, or spiritual life? If so, can you reasonably add it to your schedule? You must be certain that you are busy doing the right things and not just busy doing things.

THE REWARDS
OF DISCIPLINE

Are we talking about all work and no play? Is discipline going to make your life a drudgery? Not by any means. No one enjoys his leisure and recreation more than a person of discipline. Discipline is not some sterile way of marching through life. We are talking about the joy and fulfillment of taking charge of life instead of allowing life to take charge of you. We are talking about understanding the real value behind what you have. Nothing allows you to experience the joy and beauty of living more than discipline and sacrifice. Many a parent has learned this lesson. All of us who are parents hope to give our children the best. But we also learn that to give to our children without them having to pay the price most often leaves them unappreciative. They have not discovered the value of possessions or the rewards of sacrifice.

Are you ready to tackle the task of becoming a more disciplined person? Keep your eye on the goal. Begin with some simple and obvious things in your life. Begin today. Discipline allows you to become what you want to be in character and behavior. Discipline allows you to experience life's fullest joy. Discipline is the tool in the hand of the blacksmith. You are the blacksmith. Your life is the malleable metal. Master discipline, and you will master your life.

PART THREE

THE CRUTCH OF
STATUS

Building Character & Confidence

PART THREE

"Being powerful is like being a lady.
If you have to tell people you are, you aren't."[1]
MARGARET THATCHER

You may be limping along on the crutch called status. You may be, that is, if you are average and more concerned with appearing successful than really being successful. Trying to convince others that you are successful can be a full-time job and you may have added that job to your already overloaded schedule of demands. In the process you are sabotaging your ability to realize your potential by masking the real issues of success. Undue concern with what others think of you can drain you of energy, rob you of your ability to risk, and steal your confidence. This is especially unfortunate since the image-building business never made an unsuccessful person a success. Image is fine as long as it is reflecting what you really are. Anything else is a sham.

True success is a by-product of character. There is no greater determiner of success than character. Success itself is a test of who you really are inside. Thomas Carlyle once said that adversity can be a difficult teacher, but there are a hundred men who can withstand adversity for every one that can withstand success.[2] A. P. Gouthey adds, "No one knows of what he is made until prosperity and ease try him."[3] It is not enough to ask if you have what it takes to achieve success. You must ask whether or not you have what it takes to handle the success that will come. Image will never handle those demands. True confidence and character are the only things that will.

To discover real success demands that you first throw away the temptation to build an image of success and embrace the real issues of character and confidence. We will look more in depth at three of those issues. One, sorting out the factors that determine true confidence. Two, learning that real confidence leads to building confidence in others. And three, finding the commitment to endure through obstacles in life.

7

LAYING A FOUNDATION FOR CONFIDENCE

"A happy person is not a person in a certain set of circumstances, but rather a person with a certain set of attitudes "[4]
HUGH DOWNS

ALL OF US WOULD LIKE TO be more confident and self-assured. We don't have to look far to find someone talking about the importance of self-esteem. Bookstores are brimming with books on a variety of issues regarding self-esteem and confidence, magazines are a continuous platform for the gospel of self-esteem, and newspapers and talk-shows throw in their share on the discussion. Yet despite all the attention, the search for self-confidence for many people is still elusive and frustrating. How can that be? Tragically, much of the discussion about confidence and self-esteem is only superficial. True confidence cannot be faked. We regularly see magazine articles with titles such as, "How to Shine Across a Crowded Room," and "How to Appear Confident Even When You're Not." The vast majority of these discussions are not dealing with the real issues which affect confidence and self-esteem at all. Rather, they are dealing with external and superficial issues of appearance and image.

It is important not only to appear confident and self-assured, but to have a real and solid foundation of true confidence and self-assurance. As you seek to build that foundation you will discover very quickly that there are both reliable and unreliable sources of confidence. Making sure that your sense of confidence is built on the right foundation is critical.

UNDEPENDABLE SOURCES OF CONFIDENCE

What you look like. Few would disagree that our society puts far too much emphasis on what a person looks like. We have grown accustomed to seeing a small percentage of the best looking people in the world paraded across our television screens and magazine covers as the "typical person." When you add to this scenario the amazing things that film can do to make already beautiful people even more beautiful than they are, it's not difficult at all to see how that can lead us "typical people" to feel just a little down about ourselves. We should all try to look our best, no doubt. Taking interest in our appearance does help us to feel better about ourselves, but it does nothing to deal with the root issues of confidence. And when it comes down to it, not many of us want to compete on a playing field where only a few can win.

We all know deep down that looks are superficial. Under the best of circumstances, trusting in your looks for your confidence is fleeting. Simply put, we all grow old. The skin loosens, the wrinkles expand, the body gets a little softer. As we see from the words of King Lemuel in Proverbs 31:30, "Charm can be deceptive and beauty doesn't last." It doesn't matter what you do, the effects of growing older cannot be stopped. They can be slowed through a good physical fitness agenda, proper nutritional habits, and a great attitude about life, but to base your confidence on your appearance is to fight a losing battle. Similarly, dressing for success will do little to give you real confidence. Though it is certainly true that the way you dress affects your attitudes about yourself and creates the first impression that others have of you, that is by no means the same as confidence. Confidence rises above such superficial strategies. Confidence is something much deeper and much longer-lasting than how you look. Your appearance is an undependable source of confidence.

What you have. Another frequent mistake is to base your confidence or self-esteem on what you possess. Very early in life we can begin to associate what a person has with what a person is worth. The most popular kids are often the ones with the best toys and the biggest toy boxes. It is amazing how quickly our kids begin to compare what they are wearing with what their friends are wearing. We grow up wanting to dress in certain ways, cut our hair in certain styles, and be seen riding on certain types of bicycles. Soon bicycles turn into cars, and the race to better the other guy is in its adolescent full swing. Why? Because we want to be liked, and, if we are really lucky, we might even be popular.

Characteristically many of us "kids" carry these sophomoric attitudes right into adulthood and even try to bolster our level of confidence through expensive and extravagant toys, big houses, and impressive wardrobes. When Jim began working for a large California utility, he received a humorous education on gaining status among his peers. He had been promoted to the downtown Los Angeles headquarters. Not long after arriving, the offices were remodeled, and the employees were notified that they would be moving upstairs. One early morning he spotted the department head wielding a measuring tape and measuring his soon-to-be office. He seemed quite distressed, and Jim asked what was wrong. The boss said his office, though the nicest and most centrally located, was not the largest one. Later that day the staff were notified that their move would be delayed. It appears that the boss had to modify a couple of offices so that they would be smaller than his. The carpenters were coming back in to make the necessary adjustments to this catastrophic discovery. What a tragedy it is to associate what you have with what you are worth as a person. It never helps to compare. There will always be someone bigger, stronger, and faster. If not now, there will be later. A nagging lack of self-esteem will never be repaired by anything you can purchase or any symbols of status which surround you.

You've likely heard about the young businessman who was on the fast track to success. Everything seemed to be going well one crisp autumn day as he drove up I-80 on his way to a relaxing weekend in Tahoe. Suddenly he lost control. His car began to slide, and he slammed into the median. Spinning out of control, he hit two cars and smashed into the embankment before coming to a stop. As he knelt dazed and bleeding on the roadside, a police officer approached to hear him sobbing, "My BMW, my BMW. I've lost my BMW." Alarmed, the officer responded, "Sir, you should forget your BMW. Did you know you've lost your left arm?" In shock and disbelief the young businessman cried, "My Rolex! My Rolex!"

A silly anecdote like that not only reminds you of the shallowness of materialism, but is also a timely warning that your confidence must be rooted in more than what you possess if for no other reason than the simple fact that you can potentially lose every possession you own. History is replete with examples of men and women who lost everything they had. The Bible says, "Confidence placed in riches comes to nothing" (PROVERBS 11:7 GN). There is nothing wrong with owning lots of nice things as long as those things don't become the source of your identify. You want your sense of confidence and worth to be something which is secure and persevering, not something as transient and temporary as possessions. Real confidence is solid and firm!

What you've done. As great as accomplishment is, it is no substitute for real confidence either. Degrees and plaques strung across your walls may make you look and feel successful and self-assured, but it is only a facade of true confidence.

The common denominator of all these undependable sources of confidence is that they can all be outdone. There will always be someone who is more attractive, who has more and nicer stuff, and who has achieved more in less time than you. Lasting confidence doesn't put its faith in anything so fleeting and uncertain. True confidence must stand the test of time and circumstances. It must be built on a foundation that can't be stripped away by anyone or anything. If you suffer a lack of confidence, the reason may be that you have built all or a part of your self-worth on the faulty and undependable foundation of your appearance, your possessions, and your attainments. We deserve better. Your success in achieving your potential demands better. If you are to reach your full potential, you must begin to look to some dependable and lasting sources of building confidence.

DEPENDABLE SOURCES OF SELF-CONFIDENCE

What does it mean to develop true confidence which is built on dependable sources? How do you move beyond merely treating the symptoms and deal with the issues that really affect confidence? Our belief is that confidence is first and foremost a spiritual issue. The Bible says, "Reverence for the Lord gives confidence and security to a man and his family" (PROVERBS 14:26 GN). Confidence is a spiritual issue because it has nothing to do with the tangible and everything to do with intangibles. That's what you're admitting when you agree that confidence can't be determined by how you look, what you own, or how much you've accomplished. Confidence goes deeper. It is much more significant. You've seen that discipline can be difficult to achieve. Similarly, attempts to gain confidence can also be quite elusive. To find it, you must first understand from where confidence comes. When you have it, it will become one of your most priceless assets. You will develop true confidence when you get a handle on these important concepts.

YOU ARE A UNIQUE CREATION

In 1978, Jim's southern California church was raising money to build a new children's wing to their facilities. To kick off the program the church planned to hold a banquet on the beautiful Queen Mary in Long Beach. The pastor asked Jim's five-year-old daughter Megan to sing a solo for the event to highlight the children of the church. It was a frightening thought to a five-year-old to sing before 300 adults, but she agreed. She practiced diligently and when the big night came, she was ready. She stood before the crowd, sang beautifully, and received a standing ovation with her proud parents leading the applause.

It was certainly a confidence builder for a young girl to do so well in such a pressure filled moment. But it was the words which she had memorized and sung so beautifully that may have had the most long-term significance. The words echo the hope that all parents long for their children to believe and internalize about themselves.

I Am A Promise [5]

I am a promise, I am a possibility,
I am a promise with a capital "P";
I'm a promise to be, anything God wants me to be.

I am a promise, I am a possibility;
I am a promise with a capital "P",
I am a great big bundle of potentiality.
And I am learnin' to hear God's voice
And I am tryin' to make the right choices.
I'm a promise to be anything God wants me to be.

I can go anywhere that He wants me to go,
I can be anything that He wants me to be,
I can climb the high mountains;
I can cross the wide sea,
I'm a great big promise, you see!

I am a promise, I am a possibility;
I am a promise with a capital "P".
I am a great big bundle of potentiality.
And I am learnin' to hear God's voice

And I am tryin' to make the right choices.
I'm a promise to be anything God wants me to be.

I'll keep on list'nin' to hear God's voice,
I'll keep on tryin' to make the right choices;
I'm a promise to be anything God wants me to be.
I'm a promise to be anything He wants me to be.

God only knows how much impact that song had on young Megan's life. One thing we do know is that today that cute five-year-old girl is now a beautiful young lady. A soon-to-be college graduate with a degree, of all things, in communications, she is well on her way to reaching the potential she had sung about eighteen years earlier. Coincidence? I don't think so. As my good friend John White so often reminds me: "The definition of coincidence is God working anonymously!"

The earlier we realize the uniqueness of who we are, the sooner we will develop real-life confidence. To have confidence you must be happy with who you are—not just what you look like, but who you really are. Few of us carry around the right understanding of all God created us to be. Each of us is incredibly unique. How original are you? Scientists tell us that molecules called DNA determine the unique qualities of each of us, from the size of our noses, to the length of our legs, to our tempers or lack thereof. Mathematicians estimate that the DNA molecule can unite in an almost infinite number of ways. To be more specific, the number of possible combinations would be ten followed by two billion, 400 million zeroes! By contrast, scientists estimate that all the atomic particles in the universe would number ten followed by seventy-six zeroes! What does all of that mean? No one has ever been, or will ever be like you. You are unique beyond comparison. Because of the way you are made, you have a contribution to make to the world that no one else could make in just the same way. You bring an uncommon mix to the table. That is reason for feeling good about yourself. You are an original.

Did you know that it would take a computer the size of several city blocks to carry out the functions of your brain? The design of your body is amazing. It is said that Charles Darwin used to wake up with a cold sweat thinking about the intricacies of the human eye. What an incredible creation you are. Dr. Harold J. Morowitz of Yale conducted a study of the human body and determined that the average-sized person is worth $6,000,015.44. That is nothing compared to the 6000 trillion dollars it would cost to create each cell of your body. As mind-boggling as those numbers are, all of it is really trivial when you realize that your worth is priceless to God. There is no dollar figure you could put on how much you mean to Him. He has gone to incredible lengths to show you that and point you to a relationship with Him. God has made you unique and valuable. That is the beginning point of confidence.

YOU HAVE SOMETHING TO OFFER THE WORLD

Have you ever come to the devastating conclusion that you don't have anything significant to offer to the world? Maybe you have a nagging doubt that your life could amount to much. Perhaps you are sometimes afraid to dream. Or you feel deep down that you don't have special abilities. How untrue! This cute and humorous poem can help all of us gain a little perspective on life.

"A Little Mixed Up"

Just a line to say I'm living,
That I'm not among the dead,
Though I'm getting more forgetful,
And more mixed up in the head.

For sometimes, I can't remember,
When I stand at the foot of the stair,
If I must go up for something,
Or I've just come down from there.

And before the 'fridge so often
My poor mind's filled with doubt.
Have I just put food away, or
Have I come to take some out?

And there's times when it is dark out,
With my night cap on my head,
I don't know if I'm retiring,
Or just getting out of bed.

So, if it's my turn to write you,
There's no need in getting sore,
I may think that I have written
And don't want to be a bore.

So, remember, I do love you,
And I wish that you were here,
But now it's nearly mail time,
So I must say "goodbye, dear."

There I stood beside the mailbox,
With a face so very red.
Instead of mailing you my letter
I have opened it instead.

I like my bifocals,
My dentures fit me fine,
My hearing aid is perfect –
But, Lord, how I miss my mind.

Because you are made so unique in your identity, you also have unique talents and skills. God gives all of us distinctive, individual aptitudes. Sometimes those skills must be cultivated and brought out, but they are present nonetheless. It may be that a lifetime of feeling that you are unexceptional has buried those latent talents deep inside. They can be rediscovered or discovered for the first time. The worst thing you can do to is convince yourself that you are ordinary. You aren't now nor were you ever ordinary, average, common, plain, or mundane. You are cheating the world if you have never discovered what your unique blend of skills and personality can bring to the people around you.

Do you know what these people have in common: Albert Einstein, Helen Keller, Albert Schweitzer, Mahatma Ghandi, Winston Churchill, Franklin D. Roosevelt? Each of these were among three hundred highly successful, accomplished people who were studied in hopes of finding their so-called secrets. The results of the study surprisingly indicated that they came from diverse backgrounds, seventy-five percent of which included some form of severe poverty, a broken home, or rejecting and domineering parents. Another twenty-five percent had a major physical handicap. They became accomplished for one reason. They compensated for their weaknesses and majored on what they could do well, rather than what they couldn't do. We're sure you are acutely aware of the things that you don't do well. Most of us could list rather easily the areas in which we wish we were better or more proficient. But could you list as easily the areas in which you have exceptional abilities and talents? Don't major on the things you do poorly. Concentrate on those positive and exceptional things which you do so well. Bet you can think of some things! If not, ask someone who loves you and will help you become all that God created you to be.

It's possible that you feel intimidated by the idea that you have unique skills and contributions to bring to the world. But the truth is that you do have abilities that you can cultivate and use to help you reach your goals and fulfill your potential. Knowing that you have unique talents can give you the confidence to keep going and be the best you can be. The bottom line is that your confidence lies in the truth that you are a uniquely original person who is of inestimable worth and has a never-before-seen combination of personality, skill, insight, and outlook that makes you valuable. No one can take that away from you. It makes no difference when you were born, what age you are, the color of your skin, where you went to school, or how much money you make. It makes no difference if you're tall, dark, and handsome, or short, pale, and so-so. Your confidence will be found in your identity. You are unique, and you have potential to make a significant impact on your world when you develop your potential to its fullest.

8

SECURING CONFIDENCE
BY GIVING IT AWAY

*"Keep away from people who try to
belittle your ambitions. Small people always
do that, but the really great make you feel
that you, too, can become great."*[1]
MARK TWAIN

AS WE HAVE SEEN, FINDING
self-esteem is an elusive quest for most. One simple reason is that
many seekers fail to take their quest for achieving confidence far
enough. Building on the right foundation of confidence is only the
beginning. You are just getting started when you feel good about
who you are and your ability to succeed. You have not truly
attained a high level of self-esteem when you merely become
confident and assured of yourself. You will have reached a high
level of self-esteem when you can build that same confidence in

people around you. That is the true test of self-esteem. You never really possess anything that you cannot give away.

The stimulating story of R.G. LeTourneau is a wonderful example of a man who embodied this principle more than anyone we know. R.G. LeTourneau persevered through many early failures to rise to worldwide eminence in manufacturing and construction. He was an industrialist whose inventiveness put him far ahead of his time. A trail blazer in producing massive equipment, he helped invent and build everything from giant bulldozers and earth-movers to mobile missile launchers. To say his exploits made him a wealthy man would be an understatement, for certain. But he is remembered not so much for the money he made, as for the money he gave away. A committed Christian man, LeTourneau gave ninety percent of his money away to help do God's work in the world. His inspiring story is a tribute to his faith as well as to his character. LeTourneau learned the lesson that we only own something that we have the capacity to give away.

If you have money but find it difficult to give any away to charity, you don't possess that money; it possesses you. Similarly, teachers will tell you that you don't really understand something until you can adequately communicate it to someone else. This is a fact that is as true of confidence as of anything else. You don't possess confidence until you are able to give it to others. This is a supreme test of whether or not you are a confident person. Confidence is contagious.

Willis Reed is one of the all-time great NBA basketball players. He finished his ten-year, 650-game career with 12,183 points, 8,414 rebounds, two coveted NBA championships, two playoff MVPs, and one League MVP. Obviously, he was a pivotal member of his team whenever they took the court. In the 1970 NBA playoffs, Reed's heroics created what would become one of the great stories of sports. He had made it through several grueling playoff series with a bad left knee. In the league championship series against the Los Angeles Lakers, Reed's New York Knicks had battled to a 3-3 tie in the best-of-seven series. But going into the final, winner-take-all game, it looked as if Reed would be unable to play. His left knee was badly hurt. The team was down. The fans were devastated at the news that their star center could not take the court for game seven.

On the night of the big game, the crowd at Madison Square Garden erupted when Willis Reed was seen dressed in uniform coming out of the tunnel with the rest of the team. Battling through intense pain, Reed started the game and scored the first basket. He was unable to play long. But his determination and courage inspired a confidence in his teammates that propelled them to go on and win the game and the 1970 NBA Championship. Jim has to admit that, being a Lakers fan, he couldn't enjoy the outcome of the game, but even he had to respect the courage of Willis Reed and the confidence he inspired in his fellow Knickerbockers. Your confidence has the same effect on the people who come into contact with you. Confidence is contagious. Lack of confidence is infectious. Your confidence, or your lack of it, will rub off on everyone around you.

REALIZING HOW MUCH YOU AFFECT OTHERS

We read of an author, Mark Littleton, who once had a friend impact him with these words: "Be kind. Everyone you meet is fighting a hard battle. There are people everywhere in need of a good word, an uplifting comment to fire their hopes and dreams." Daily you come into contact with people just like that. People all around you need a boost of confidence that you have the power to give or to withhold. Confident people make a lifestyle out of giving those good words to others in all their relationships. A mark of high self-esteem is the ability to gain satisfaction from seeing others around you succeed. That takes a high degree of security, and not many ever reach that level. Those with low levels of self-esteem want those around them to do just a little worse than they, thereby validating their own success.

But people with high levels of self-esteem can feel secure, even excited about helping someone else achieve at even greater levels than themselves. You know that you have arrived when you are able to build confidence and esteem in others. If you are confident in your abilities, you are not insecure in helping others around you become better. If you are confident in who you are, you can be secure enough to build in others a sense of confidence in who they are. If that is a goal that you would like to achieve, here are some suggestions which we believe will help you get there.

UNDERSTANDING THE POWER OF YOUR WORDS

In the cultures of Bible times, as in many Eastern cultures to this day, there was something mysteriously powerful about words. In Bible days it was common practice for the Hebrew father, shortly before his death, to give a verbal blessing to his eldest son. This blessing was seen as empowering the son to continue in the prosperity the father had enjoyed through his long life. There is quite an interesting story in Genesis 27 about an aging father named Isaac who was deceived by his younger son Jacob into giving his blessing to him, instead of to his older son Esau. When Isaac found out, he was, of course, furious at having had been deceived by Jacob.

The most curious aspect of the story, at least for those of us with Western mindsets, is that Isaac did not simply revoke the blessing. If it were us, we would have said, "No, that didn't count. You tricked me, and the blessing is void." But Isaac didn't renounce his blessing. Some might blame it on the ignorance of an ancient mindset. But the facts don't support that conclusion. It is only in relatively modern times that we have lost that concept of the tremendous power of words. Quite frankly, we take words very lightly these days. In commenting on the power of our words the Bible author James says, "Men control the movements of a large animal like the horse with a tiny bit placed in its mouth .... The human tongue is physically small, but what tremendous effects it can boast of,"[2] (JAMES 3:3,5 PH).

Words are units of energy, and when they are spoken they impact wherever they fall. Craig was once affected by a poem that he read as a college student. To this day he carries it in his memory as a reminder of the awesome power of his own words.

> *Little boys flying kites pull in their white-winged birds,*
> *This you cannot do, when you are flying words.*
> *Thoughts unexpressed may someday fall back dead,*
> *But God himself can't kill words once they're said.*

When you speak, you create good will or bad. You can create peace or conflict. You can instruct or confuse. But whatever you do, when you speak you do something. Words carry life. We know of people in the middle years of life who are still feeling the effects of the words of someone who hurt them as a young child. Forty-year-old words still are loaded with power. By the same token, we know of people who consistently persevere in life because of someone who once said, "I know you can do it!" Understanding the tremendous power of your words can and should cause you to reflect on exactly what you are creating with your tongue each day.

In the fall of 1992, Jim's son Andrew was a 15-year-old sophomore tailback on his high school junior varsity football team. Jim had been invited by a good friend, Jim Stump, Chaplain of the Stanford football team, to speak to the team at a Chapel Service prior to their game. Andrew joined his dad on the two and one half hour drive from Sacramento to Palo Alto. Following the Chapel Service, they both received sideline passes which allowed them to watch the game from the vantage point of the coaches and players. During the third quarter, a Stanford tailback was running down the sidelines when two linebackers knocked him out of bounds just ten yards or so from where Jim and Andrew were standing. The size and speed of all three players resulted in a tremendous collision, and as Jim glanced toward Andrew he saw an expression of wide-eyed amazement on his son's face.

Later, while driving home, Jim asked Andrew if he enjoyed the day. "Yea," Andrew replied, "It was great." Then Jim asked, "Can you picture yourself doing that someday?" Andrew's response surprised Jim a bit. He said, "Get real dad, I'll never be that good." Jim told him that he believed he could be as good as he wanted to be, if he was willing to work hard enough.

Two years later, that day was repeated in an almost uncanny way. Andrew was now a 17-year-old high school senior tailback, Jim was asked again to speak at the chapel service and they both ended up on the same field watching a Stanford tailback running down the sidelines at nearly the exact spot as before. As in the game two years earlier, two huge linebackers crushed the Stanford tailback out of bounds near where Jim and Andrew were standing. However, when Jim glanced over to see Andrew's reaction this time, Andrew calmly looked at his dad and said, "The guy should have cut in."

What a difference in attitude and perspective.

What are you doing to and for the lives of those who hear your voice? Are they better off or worse off by having listened to you? There is tremendous power in your words. Are you using that power to build the confidence of those with whom you talk each day?

GIVING ATTENTION TO YOUR THOUGHT LIFE

Confident people are positive people. They are happy, encouraged, and enthusiastic, and they find it natural to impart that to others. When people are negative, critical, and discouraging, it is most often because they are feeling that way themselves. Hurting people hurt people. You change those habits of speaking as you change your habits of thinking. Jesus said, "Out of the overflow of the heart the mouth speaks" (MATTHEW 13:34 NIV). That truth of Jesus is now generally understood and accepted by behavioral scientists and motivators everywhere. Your behavior is a direct result of what is happening inside you. The way you think impacts the way you feel, which in turn impacts the way you act and speak. To help people out of depression, many counselors have reversed this process, in a procedure known as cognitive therapy, to teach the simple truth that you can change the way you feel by changing the way you think. You are not a prisoner to your feelings, you are not a prisoner to your habits, and you are not a prisoner to a negative and unhelpful thought life.

How do you think when confronted with a challenging situation? How do you react mentally when you are criticized or when things don't work out as you hoped? What do you think about during those dead times in your daily schedule? Where does your mind run when confronted with a challenging temptation? Too often you may feel that you can't change the way you think. You can! Your thinking is driven by what you feed your mind. Determine what your daily diet is for your mind, and you will discover the secret to bringing your thought life under your control again. Change your diet, and you change your feelings and your actions. You can become an encouraging person who instills confidence in others. It all begins with the commitment to monitor what you feed your mind.

You live in the real world, and you have to learn how to counterattack all those images which don't support your values. To help you with that, we have a specific plan. We practice a daily time of reading the Bible. We would recommend that for you as well. If you are new to Bible study, begin in the New Testament books. Visit a Christian bookstore and ask for a translation of the Bible that you can understand with ease. We make a regular practice of reading instructional and motivational books on character, spiritual growth, attitude, goals, leadership development, family, and personal growth. We listen to good positive speakers in person and on tape both on topics that instruct and inspire us in our given fields, and about Christian living in general. We work hard at watching our vocabulary for patterns of negative speaking, the first indication of negative and destructive thinking patterns. All of these things can help you become a better builder of confidence in others.

LOOKING FOR THE
BEST IN EVERYONE

Few of the Bible's authors surpass James in directness and relevance. At one point in his letter, James says to his readers, "Dear brothers, don't be too eager to tell others their faults, for we all make many mistakes" (JAMES 3:1 LB). We like the translation of that same verse which says, "Don't be self-constituted censors and reprovers of others"³ Anybody can see the faults in others, and it is easy to be a critic. It doesn't take much depth or thought to constantly look for and find the worst in people. What takes diligent and faithful attention is cultivating the ability to look for and find the best in others.

Peter is one of the most loved and well-known men of the Bible. The reason is likely that when we are first introduced to him, he is most noted for his blunders and mistakes. Peter was a classic case of someone who could always be counted on to say the wrong thing at the wrong time. He was the epitome of inconsistency and undependability. It was easy to find the faults in Peter, and no doubt the other eleven Apostles did just that. We can imagine the ribbing that Peter must have taken from his buddies when he repeatedly blundered and dropped the ball. But Jesus, who of course was acutely aware of Peter's faults, chose instead to major on the strengths of Peter. One day, as we read in Chapter 16 of Matthew, when Peter had an uncharacteristically good and astute observation, Jesus told Peter that He was giving him a new name. He would no longer be called Simon (as he had previously been known), but would be called Peter (as we know him now).

Jesus went on to describe that the name Peter meant "Rock," and He was naming him such because he one day would become a strong and dynamic leader in the newly forming Church.

Peter was anything but a rock, but Jesus saw in him hidden potential to which others were blind. He didn't see a bungling underachiever who too often engaged his mouth before engaging his brain. Jesus instead chose to see the potential dynamic leader who would be instrumental in converting thousands of people to Christianity through his stirring oratory and dynamic, charismatic personality. To look for the best in others means that you choose to major on strengths rather than become preoccupied by shortcomings. Yet you cannot do that until you first have grown to like yourself. As you have seen in previous chapters, as long as you don't feel good about your own strengths and competencies, you will always be threatened by the strengths of others. You are growing in your own confidence when you can look for the best in those around you.

EXPECTING THE BEST OF EVERYONE

A critical spirit not only gives evidence of a low self-image, it is certainly not the best way to influence people to change. To point out someone's faults often just causes that person to become defensive and closed to real change. People tend to live up to our expectations of them.

Alan Loy McGinnis showed this fact dramatically in his book *Bringing Out the Best in People*. He cites a study by Harvard psychologist Robert Rosenthal and San Francisco school principle Lenore Jacobson which dramatically demonstrates the effect of expectation on people's actions. Kids at the test school were given aptitude tests, and the next fall the teachers were given the names of several students in each class who possessed exceptional learning potential. What the teachers didn't know was that the test results had been rigged, and these "high achieving students" had been picked completely at random. At year end all of the children were re-tested. The results: those who were expected to achieve did just that. In fact, they had gained an average of 15 to 27 IQ points. It was the positive attitude toward them that led to the growth in these students.

Leadership author Warren Bennis recounts a similar experiment where people were given puzzles to solve. Each were then given fictitious results. Half were told that they had done well, while the other half were told they had done poorly. When they were later given a second test they did as well or as poorly as they had been told they did on the first test. You can then conclude that you can have a significant effect on the people around you by your attitude toward them and your expectations of them. When you expect the people in your life to be losers, and when you communicate that through attitude and through your words, they very likely will become losers. On the other hand, when you expect people to be winners, and when you communicate that verbally and nonverbally, you can actually help them to become the winners that they are.

Again, that type of positive attitude can only develop when you feel good about yourself. But no matter what, begin looking for and expecting the best in others today. When you do, something terrific will begin happening in your life. Developing that attitude toward others not only reflects your positive self-esteem. It will help you build it.

NEVER GIVING UP
ON PEOPLE

Everyone drops the ball somewhere along the way. When someone you know is down because of failure, you have an awesome responsibility to him. You can help shape his future by your attitude towards him in that most critical time. When your friend knows that you believe in him and will not give up on him, he gets tremendous empowerment to go on. You help him build his view of himself and his potential. As you have seen, Jesus is the Master of building positive self-esteem in others.

Think for a minute about Jesus and all of the disciples. Jesus recruited twelve men who hardly would have made anyone's list of future movers and shakers. They were a rough crew of men from a variety of backgrounds. All had extremely rough edges, and they seemed to show few signs of progress in the time Jesus spent with them. They repeatedly failed in their assigned tasks, denied Him when the pressure was on, and, after three years of constant association with Jesus, failed to really understand who He was or what His mission was. But Jesus never gave up on them, and it was His unwavering belief in them that helped shape them into the world movers they would eventually become. With the exception of one who died of natural causes, each of the remaining faithful disciples died the death of a martyr. Their faith and commitment would not be shaken. They succeeded in helping spread the Christian faith to all of the known world.

There are people in your life who need to know that you believe in them. When you take hold of that belief in people, what a powerful force you can be in the lives of those around you. One of our favorite stories illustrates the point better than we can communicate it ourselves. In his early years, the great American author Nathaniel Hawthorne one day came home a discouraged and defeated man. He informed his wife that he had been fired from his job. To his surprise she did not react with disappointment, but with joy. "Now," she said, "you can write your book!" Trying to bring her back to reality he retorted, "Yes, and what shall we live on while I am writing it?" Calmly she walked to a nearby desk and retrieved a substantial amount of money. When asked where it came from, she answered, "I have always known that you were a man of genius. I knew that someday you would write a masterpiece. So every week out of the money you have given me for housekeeping, I have saved something; here is enough to last for one more year." No price could be put on that kind of confidence and trust. What did that love and trust in her husband accomplish? Nathaniel Hawthorne used that time to write one of the great novels of all time, *The Scarlet Letter*.[4] To give that kind of gift to the people you know will be the ultimate test of your own self-confidence.

9

CONQUERING THE
TEMPTATION TO QUIT

"Nothing in the world can take the place of perseverance.
Talent will not; nothing is more common than unsuccessful men
with talent. Genius will not; unrewarded genius is almost a proverb.
Persistence and determination alone are omnipotent."[1]
CALVIN COOLIDGE

IMAGINE THAT YOUR SOLE
responsibility today was to take an inventory of your personal life.
Everything else was put on hold for the ominous task of reviewing
and surveying the steps your life has taken since the day you
entered the world. One by one the events and decisions, the relationships and the emotions play themselves out in your memory.
What do you look back on and wish you had never quit? Is it
those piano lessons, that relationship, your education, the lost
business opportunity? It is likely that there may well be many

things that you regret having quit. If the truth were known you may this very moment be on the verge of quitting something for which you will later be sorry. Failing to persevere is often the reason for a lack of self-esteem. There is no basis in the belief that you don't have talents or skill; you simply give up before you develop them fully. It is not that you can't accomplish the things that you would like to, you just quit too soon. The quality of endurance is a cornerstone of your confidence because it is often only through endurance that you see tangible growth in our latent skills and accomplishments.

Of all the qualities that help you reach your potential, one stands tall above the rest. Knowledge, motivation, discipline, and the many other important qualities for success will all fall silent and empty without the character trait of endurance. Tenacity, stamina, and determination create confidence, while quitting kills it. The greatest thing about endurance is that anyone can do it! We all begin at the same starting line. The ultimate reward for all of your work is often discovered only when you have persevered. To use a well-worn cliche: you must develop the character which stubbornly refuses to throw in the towel.

You may recognize this man, perhaps not by this synopsis of his life events, but you will know him well by name. At age 22, he failed in a business venture. At age 23, he ran for the legislature, and he was defeated. One year later he failed again in business. At age 25, he was elected to the legislature, only to have it followed one year later by the tragic death of his sweetheart. Then, at the age of 29, he was defeated for speaker, and again at age 31, he was defeated for elector. At age 34, he was defeated for Congress, and finally, at age 37, he was elected to Congress. Again, at age 39, he was defeated for Congress, and five years later he was defeated for

Senate. At age 47, he was defeated for Vice-President, and at age 49, he was once again defeated for Senate. At the age of 51, Abraham Lincoln was elected President of the United States.

Can you imagine what the media would do to an Abraham Lincoln these days? Many would think him an idiot to keep trying through all of that adversity. On the contrary, it was because of his character of endurance that Abraham Lincoln became one of America's greatest presidents and most influential men. Fathers through the decades have used Lincoln to motivate their sons. One such father was scolding his son about a bad report card. He asked his son, "Do you know what Abraham Lincoln was doing when he was your age?" "No," replied the son, "But I know what he was doing when he was your age!" As well-worn as it is, the story of Lincoln is still inspiring.

It is quite humorous to see how others have evaluated people who later became legendary leaders and success stories. In 1905 the University of Bern rejected a Ph.D. Dissertation, saying it was irrelevant and fanciful. Earlier in his career this same student was evaluated by a teacher, "He doesn't wear socks and forgets to cut his hair. Could be mentally retarded."[2] Albert Einstein persevered. An "expert" once said of this young coach, "He possesses minimal football knowledge. Lacks motivation."[3] Vince Lombardi persevered. In 1954, the then manager of the Grand Ole Opry, fired this young performer after one performance saying, "You ain't goin' nowhere . . . son. You ought to go back to drivin' a truck."[4] Elvis Presley persevered. The more you study men and women who have actualized their dreams, the more you discover that the end result is often brought about by dogged determination, unswerving perseverance, and stubborn endurance. William Feather once said, "Success seems to be largely a matter of hanging on after others have let go."[5] If anything can give you the strength and motivation to get back on the horse and not quit, that should.

Paul Harvey, who says everything well, says, "If there is one common denominator of men whom the world calls successful it is this: They get up when they fall down."[6] The Bible writer James summed it up himself when he penned these words, "Perseverance must finish its work so that you may be mature and complete, not lacking anything" (JAMES 1:4 NIV). That is endurance. It is the ultimate test of character. Anyone can be disciplined for a day, or a week, or a month. But only someone with the character of endurance can parley that discipline into success over the long haul. Anyone can have confidence in the middle of easy times. But only endurance will allow you to maintain confidence through the failures and rejections. Anyone can maintain their relationships for a few weeks, months, or even years, but only endurance can maintain them for a lifetime. Anything else you do will prove itself worthless, unless that type of endurance becomes a part of who you are and how you operate.

It is always easier to quit than to persevere . . . in the short run. But endurance pays huge dividends over the long haul. What kind of reputation will you build? Will you be known as a flash in the pan person or will you be known as someone who finished the race? How do you want to be remembered? Roberto Duran is without doubt one of the top fighters who ever put on a pair of boxing gloves. His record in the boxing ring already had him destined to be called one of the greatest fighters ever. He was known to have "fists of stone," and he destroyed his opponents. But regardless of his championships, Roberto Duran will likely be remembered by many as the one who taught everyone the meaning of the phrase "no mas." Duran had already given Sugar

Ray Leonard his only defeat. But this June night in 1980 was an entirely different story. Leonard was frustrating Duran through his quickness and elusiveness, and in the eighth round, an apparently healthy Duran shocked everyone by saying he would take "no more" from his opponent Sugar Ray Leonard. Duran was quitting. Boxing enthusiasts lost respect for a great boxer who chose to quit when he could have persevered. Who would want to be remembered by such a low point in an otherwise stellar career? How can you ensure that you are developing a character which will endure? Is endurance necessary? If you have any goals, it is important. If you hope to reach your personal potential, it is a must.

IDENTIFYING YOUR PRIMARY SOURCE OF STRENGTH

We should pause here with a word of encouragement. Everyone hits a point when he wants to quit. Everyone! It's all too easy to think that people like Abraham Lincoln must have been exceptional and never wanted to quit. That is simply not the case. Many great men and women who have been honest with their struggles reveal times when they wanted to give up the fight. The Apostle Paul was a man who held disdain for quitters. The Bible records one specific episode when a young and inexperienced pastor named John Mark turned back in the face of difficulty. Paul was not exactly patient with the young man. In fact, he lashed out and told the young man he was finished in missionary circles! Later in life Paul's relationship with John Mark was restored, and likely that included generous amounts of forgiveness from both sides. One of the many lessons we that you can learn from that episode is that Paul was not a quitter.

In the twilight of his long and distinguished career, Paul waxed philosophical as he reflected on his wealth of challenges, victories, pitfalls, and accomplishments. At the end of his life, Paul said with pride that he could look back knowing that when all was said and done, he had fought the good fight and finished the race (2 TIMOTHY 4:7). He never threw in the towel. That is quite a statement. But that in no way means Paul didn't sometimes want to quit. He did! In one of Paul's letters he records these telling words:

> We do not want you to be uninformed, brothers, about the hardships we suffered in the province of Asia. We were under great pressure, far beyond our ability to endure, so that we despaired even of life.
>
> 2 CORINTHIANS 1:8 (NIV)

None of us are immune from the pressures which pound on us and make giving in the easiest thing to do. If you noticed Paul's words, he said that his pressure was "beyond his ability to endure." Frankly speaking he is admitting that he did not have the strength within himself to keep going. It is a sign of emotional health to recognize your limitations. None of us are supermen or superwomen. You sometimes reach the limits of your endurance. Sometimes it is your ability, your patience, your focus, or your vision that cracks under the pressure. Whatever it is, the question remains, "What is it that gives me the strength to go on when the strongest of people would cave in?" In thinking about the source of your strength, there are three factors which you must consider.

DETERMINING YOUR SOURCE OF STRENGTH

To maintain the character of endurance, you must have significant resources from which to draw. "Why go through the trouble?" is a legitimate question. It takes enormous energy to endure in difficult circumstances, and without proper internal and external motivation you don't stand much of a chance. To maintain motivation, you need to have a well-defined purpose, a discernible sense of priorities, and a strong wealth of resources.

YOUR PURPOSE

First let's discuss purpose. The motivations of achieving people are as diverse as the number of people who achieve. We once heard a physician say that the reason she went into medicine was that her parents laughed at her when she said, at age twelve, that she wanted to be a doctor. Determined to prove them wrong, she persisted. That's certainly not an ideal motivation for being a doctor. No one can really be happy whose prime motivation is to prove someone else wrong. Yet it does illustrate the point that we are all driven by some purpose to accomplish things or to simply persist in trying circumstances. What is that purpose for you? Is it your family? Is it your career or monetary goals? Is it some humanitarian project you would like to see become reality? Maybe your purpose would be that of the Apostle Paul's, that his hope was found in his relationship with God. As for us, we have found that this is the only sense of purpose which transcends all situations and gives us a sense of personal peace and satisfaction. Whether you have yet made that discovery or not, determining your purpose in each area of life will help you cultivate the character of endurance. When the rubber hits the road, you need to know what keeps you going.

YOUR PRIORITIES

Priorities are equally important. Achieving people can easily become driven people. Being overly driven, for instance, to attain career goals can demolish families, personal health, personal values, or emotional well-being. Any good thing out of balance becomes negative. That is why it is essential that you have a very specific and heartfelt sense of what is really important in life. Arranging your priorities is important. Even more important is determining what that arrangement of priorities will mean to the way you live your life. Jim says that his top four priorities are: 1) God; 2) Family; 3) Country; 4) Career. That kind of understanding of what is most important to you is necessary. Can you delineate the most important things in your life and the order of their importance? Without that you are like a ship without a rudder or a Ferrari without a full tank of gas. Your priorities fuel what your life will become. Can you rattle off the six most important things in your life right now? If you struggle with that, take time now to make those important designations. It may make all the difference.

But even more important than knowledge of a list of priorities is a firm understanding of what that will mean in your everyday life. What does it mean to put God first, and how will that impact your weekly schedule, your finances, and your personal relationships? What does it really mean to say that family is more important to you than your career? How does that impact your performance objectives at work, and what will that mean to the way you make decisions about your future? It is easy to list priorities on paper, but it is much more challenging to actually consider how that will play itself out in your life. The truth is that your priorities (whether they are known to you or not) lie behind nearly every decision you make.

Sometimes priorities are dynamic. They can ebb and flow at various stages of life. During certain times of the year our career responsibilities may supersede our family time. A family crisis may put work on the back burner even though the financial cost is high. But because we understand what is really important to us, we are able to keep perspective, and our life stays in balance. Priorities give our life boundaries. The natural thing to happen in life is that those things which are the most pressing become the highest priority. Though inevitably situations arise which are beyond our control, our priorities allow us to bounce back. They keep us from straying so far that one day we look up and wonder how we got over here. Our priorities are foundations on which we build our life.

YOUR RESOURCES

We have each owned diesel cars. Because only a few stations in town carry diesel, it sometimes creates problems for the diesel owner. If his tank is treading the empty line, the gas station on the corner is worthless to him if it only carries leaded and unleaded gasoline. Complicating the situation is the fact that if his diesel car runs out of fuel, he doesn't simply get towed to the nearest diesel station. He gets towed to the nearest diesel service center to get the fuel pump re-primed. As a result, he learns to plan re-fueling stops much more carefully than he otherwise might. He knows the location of every station which has a diesel pump, because he doesn't want to run dry.

There are also times when your personal tank can run dangerously low. You need to know where the stations are so you can have your spirits renewed, your motivation empowered, and your energy recharged. You don't want to run dry. Regular exercise, fellowship with friends, weekends away, or whatever works to keep your tank filled, needs to become the rule and not simply the exception. Unless you become consistently recharged you will not be able to endure when the going gets tough.

You remember our friend the Apostle Paul. It is interesting to note that when he felt he didn't have the ability to go on, he credited his endurance to the supernatural strength God gave him. Paul is not the only one to make that claim. We like to keep track of as many inspiring stories as we can. It is a great help to us personally to hear of those who have beaten the odds, done the undoable, and discovered their personal strength to endure. No story tops that of Dave Dravecky and his journey through professional baseball.

Growing up, Dave dreamed about being Sandy Koufax. He imagined himself blowing fastballs by major league sluggers, just like Sandy. He was one of the lucky ones who saw his boyhood dream turn into reality when he was drafted by professional baseball's San Diego Padres. He was later traded to the San Francisco Giants, and in his own words he says, "I was playing in the big leagues and being paid a big-league salary. I had a wonderful wife and two terrific kids. I was living my dream. But then something went wrong."[7] Indeed, something went very wrong. A small lump on his pitching arm turned out to be cancer. In cutting out the tumor the surgeon was also forced to take out much of the muscle that made Dave a great major league pitcher.

The doctors said he would never pitch again. He would be lucky to play catch with his son, the doctors said. Dravecky proved them wrong. In his book *Comeback,* he chronicles the amazing story of how his faith and perseverance brought him back to the big leagues. On August 10, 1989, Dave miraculously pitched once more against the Cincinnati Reds. What a day it was. Five days later, the joy was gone. We remember watching the news that day. The highlights showed the last pitch that Dave Dravecky ever threw. It was the one that caused his arm to break with a crack so loud that it was heard up through the stands. It was an agonizing moment. We all cried with Dave that day. But Dave did not let discouragement stop him. He was not a quitter. He would come back, again. Dave witnessed his teammates win the National League championship game that sent them to the World Series. Then another tragedy. Though his arm was in a sling, he got caught up in the celebration. He was bumped from behind, and his arm was broken for a second time.

Dave was forced to retire, and he later found that the cancer had returned to his arm. Complications mounted, and his arm grew worse. Having exhausted all options, Dave Dravecky was left with the horrifying reality that his arm would need to be amputated. The arm that was the central focus of his life and career was gone. In his second book, Dravecky writes, "What do you do when you can't come back? Sooner or later that's a question we all have to face. For me it just happened to be sooner."[8] Through all of this tragedy Dave speaks openly about his faith in God which gave him the strength to endure.

Throughout history and even today millions have credited their ability to endure to their personal relationship with God. Wherever yours comes from, you need resources that you know are powerful and dependable. For some unexplainable reason, when you need endurance the most is when you often find filling stations to be farthest away. Endurance is the blue-collar work of success. To make it work, you need to be sure of your purpose, your priorities, and your resources.

CONQUERING QUITTING POINTS

All the rhetoric aside. What do you do when every ounce of energy in you is loudly crying, "Quit?" We have both counseled with people who were on the verge of making a major life decision. It is amazing that often those decisions are not based on the facts or on rational thinking, and often any counsel we give falls on deaf ears. Why does that happen? Are these irrational people who don't have access to the facts? Not at all. They are simply normal people like all of us are who are sometimes driven by pure emotion which says, "I can't keep going." What can you do? You can learn to break past those invisible but very real barriers known as quitting points.

Nearly all disciplines have a quitting point. One of the most dramatic is found through what some long-distance runners experience. The twenty-six-mile marathon race is one of the most intense tests of the limits of human endurance. Many a runner will testify that during a race he must often break through what he calls "the wall." The wall in a point is the race when he feels like he can't possibly go on. Every muscle and bone in his body aches and cries out for rest. Every step is a chore, and the thought of finishing the remaining miles is agonizing. The body physiologically experiences an amazing phenomenon. When the runner finally breaks through that wall, there is a new burst of life and energy. He discovers the mythical second wind. Having broken through that quitting point, he can go on to finish the race with strength and vigor.

Life is like that. When you learn to break through relational, spiritual, and professional quitting points, you discover a new sense of energy and strength which you never knew existed. At a quitting point you come face to face with a challenge. Will you retreat and settle for what life has to offer this side of the wall, or will you cross over those quitting points to discover a whole new world of accomplishment and satisfaction?

Few people realize the incredible price men and women have had to pay in the past just for the privilege of following their faith. The Apostle John dealt personally with people in that position every day of his life. In the last book of the Bible which he wrote, he describes this amazing situation:

> *The people of God who are destined for prison will be*
> *arrested and taken away; those destined for death will*
> *be killed But do not be dismayed, for here is your*
> *opportunity for endurance and confidence.*
> REVELATION 13:10 (LB)

You may want to take notice of the phrase "here is your opportunity." You may be wondering what he is talking about. These are ordinary people faced with the very real possibility of imprisonment or death, and John calls this an opportunity? John understood very well the concept of quitting points. Certainly if anyone has felt like giving in to fear, these people would. But John encourages them to use this opportunity to develop confidence that comes from not falling to the temptation to give up the fight. You see, someone can take away just about everything you have, including your family, your money, or your job. You could even lose your country or your health, but no one could ever take away your will to endure . . . except you. The key to endurance is to recognize and commit to conquer the quitting points in your life.

One of the problems in our culture is that we tend to idealize and dramatize quitting points. In relationships, you may reason that if you can't continue with one, you'll just start over with another one. The problem is, you will never deal with the root causes of your failed relationships until you commit to break through the quitting points. You may fantasize about quitting your job or cheer when the big screen actor tells his boss to "take this job and shove it!" But rarely do the movies continue the story with the struggles that remain to pay the bills and feed the family. Academically, you may feel that you don't have the time, energy, or motivation to finish that college degree. That may be your quitting point that spoils your opportunity for career advancement and erodes your self-esteem. Spiritually, you may not feel that you can experience a vigorous and meaningful faith that some others seem to possess. That is a quitting point which keeps many from diligently seeking what God offers to all of us. Life is filled with quitting points.

People sometimes quit after they have reached a certain level of success. Have you settled for good rather than striving for the best? You may have discovered your quitting point. This is often a weakness in your character that allows you to give in rather than persevere. Achievement, success, and reaching our greatest potential will never happen until you commit to making endurance the legacy which defines your character, no matter what. Giving up and self-confidence are incompatible character traits. When you quit, your confidence in yourself takes the hardest blow. If we could accomplish anything through this book, we would hope that it might encourage one person to persevere when he would have otherwise given up.

PART FOUR

THE CRUTCH OF
DOUBT

Amplifying Your Personal Vision

PART FOUR

"We all have possibilities we don't know about.
We can do things we don't know about.
We can do things we don't even dream we can do."[1]
DALE CARNEGIE

As a high school senior in 1960, Jim reached the finals for the California state wrestling championship. There is no more pure competition than the struggle of one man against another in the classic art of wrestling. Two competitors stare each other down, armed with nothing but their own muscle and a desire to win. It is two wills locked in a battle of skill and power as both seek to pin the other to the mat. It is not much different as you wrestle with reaching your personal potential in life. You must develop your skills, build your determination, and make the commitment to be the best you possibly can. There will be defeats along the way, but you must persevere. In that journey, you can throw away the crutch of ignorance, becoming a growing person. You can toss the crutch of laziness as you become lean and disciplined. You can cast off the crutch of status while you develop true confidence and endurance. Still, you have not equipped yourself with all the needed techniques for winning the battle to realize your potential. You still may find yourself hung up and stifled by the crutch that we call doubt.

Doubt is that nagging belief that you can never be what you hoped. Like the triathlete with his shoelaces tied together, you are held back by doubt from running the race towards achievement. Doubt is like that doggedly determined entrepreneur we heard about recently. Having returned from his Caribbean cruise, he tragically fell off the ramp upon leaving the ship. While the crew frantically worked to find a lifeline to throw to him, the stunned observers watched him sink under the water and reappear three separate times. Before going under for the fourth time, he could be heard to scream, "If someone doesn't get me a rope . . . I'm going to have to let go of my suitcases!" Doubt can cripple an otherwise well-conditioned achiever and make reaching our personal potential beyond reach.

There is only one solution for doubt—it is called vision. God created you with vision as the foundation. What you achieve will in large measure depend on your ability to harness and direct the power of your personal vision. Toward that end, let's examine first how to increase our capacity for personal vision. Secondly, you'll discover the power of vision. And finally, let's discuss how to carve out a unique vision for your life.

10

CULTIVATING YOUR CAPACITY FOR PERSONAL VISION

"Every man takes the limits of his own field of vision for the limits of the world."[2]
SCHOPENHAUER

ONE OF THE MOST DIVERSE and talented people in history was Benjamin Franklin. His accomplishments throughout his more than eighty years of life are legendary. He was a printer, philanthropist, statesman, scientist, and inventor. In Europe he was known as a symbol of enlightenment and freedom. He invented a heating stove and bifocals, and the lightning rod was his idea. He refused to have any of his inventions patented so that everyone could profit from them. His long lifetime of achievements exemplified his adage that the biggest tragedy of life is that most people are dead at age 28 and are buried at age 68. Unfortunately, it is true that most people have lost their dreams by the time they pass their third decade of life, and they simply spend their last four decades going through the motions. What a sad thought. But Franklin proved it doesn't have to be that way. Why was he so successful? He simply never lost his appetite for learning or his dream for accomplishing great things in life. Franklin was a man of vision.

Henry David Thoreau once said that dreams are the touchstones of our character.[3] We couldn't agree more. Vision is not a luxury for the few, it is a necessity for us all. Vision is a part of our character. It determines what we see in life. *Guideposts* magazine once related a parable of a lone shipwreck survivor on an uninhabited island. The survivor managed to build a makeshift hut in which he placed all that he had salvaged from the sinking ship. He prayed that God would send someone to rescue him and looked each day for the answer to his prayer. One day his hut erupted in flames, and he lost everything he owned. He was angry at God, who he felt had abandoned him. To the man's limited vision this was the worst thing that could have happened to him. To his surprise, the very next day a ship arrived, and the captain said, "We saw your smoke signal." Vision often sees what others refuse or fail to see. Vision always determines how you interpret what you see in life.

Vision influences what you see in life, and vision also directs where you go in life. We heard from Thoreau about the priority of vision, but he even went further: "I have learned this at least by my experiment: that if one advances confidently in the direction of his dreams and endeavors to live the life which he had imagined, he will meet with a success unexpected in common hours."[4] Most of the world's great accomplishments and discoveries came as a result of vision. Vision affects what you see and where you go in 'life, and to the extent that this is true, vision becomes another indispensable ingredient in the recipe of life.

Why is it, then, that many of us have such a difficult time obtaining vision, even in understanding it? Why do we doubt ourselves and what we can accomplish through our lives? A part of the answer is that many are struck with what we call "the Moses syndrome." The Bible chronicles the story of how God revealed to Moses that He wanted him to be the leader of the Hebrew people who would demand that Pharaoh release His people from slavery. Moses responded with serious reservations: "But Moses said to God, 'I am no great man! Why should I be the one to go to the king and lead the Israelites out of Egypt?' God said, 'I will be with you'" (EXODUS 3:11-12 EB).

As Benjamin Franklin so pointedly modeled, you can accept being ordinary and go through the motions of life, or you can choose to be a person of vision. You can be a person who carries within you the conviction that you are living to accomplish a dream. We want to share three principles which we believe will propel you toward the dynamic vision of achieving your personal potential.

PRINCIPLE #1

It is natural for you to doubt!

We can all relate to Moses. It is totally natural to doubt ourselves. A father one day was speaking to Jesus. He very much wanted to believe and follow Jesus. He had one problem. He had doubts. He said to Jesus, "I do believe. Help me overcome my unbelief!"

THROW AWAY THE CRUTCHES

(MARK 9:24 NIV). We can all identify with that man since there is not one of us who has not struggled with the issue of doubt in plenty of areas of life.

FACT #1

Everyone doubts.

All of us would like to be rid of that nemesis. We've seen that it is not comfortable or rewarding to doubt your abilities or your personality. It is not fulfilling or comforting to doubt the existence of God or your ability to have a relationship with Him. Even when you are sincerely fulfilling your life mission, doubt seems to find a way to annoy and frustrate you. Doubt can be debilitating, and it certainly is an enemy which needs to be avoided if possible and controlled at all costs.

Doubt is so damaging because it easily leads to discouragement and that can be the kiss of death. One of our favorite stories is the parable about the man who went to the devil's garage sale. At the sale the devil had all of his tools displayed on tables. Each had a price displayed on it with a red tag. The man walked past table after table of beautiful, sparkling tools with familiar names like greed, materialism, lust, lying, cheating, stealing, and so on. The tools were astonishingly reasonable in price. On one table sat a surprising tool. It was a wedge-shaped instrument labeled "discouragement." It was discolored and worn and actually appeared quite ugly. Its condition wasn't nearly as nice as the other tools, but its price was far greater than any combination of other tools on display. The man asked the devil the reason why. His response was profoundly simple. "Ah," he said. "That is my greatest and most valuable tool. No one even knows it is mine. I simply hammer away on it until I get inside a person. Once inside, I can use any of my other tools that I choose." Nothing is more damaging than discouragement. When discouraged you tend to use phrases like, "not me," "I couldn't do that," "I'm too old," "I'm too young," or "it's no use." Discouragement and doubt are partners in crime and can be our mortal enemies, foes that we all need to conquer.

But there is another side of doubt which compels us to dig deeper. While it is on one hand an enemy to be expelled, it can also be an ally to embrace. Wilson Mizner once said, "I respect faith but doubt is what gets you an education."[5] In other words, doubt is the foundation of true learning. Until we ask the right questions, we will never find the right answers. Doubt can be something immensely valuable which we all should hope to possess and cultivate. But how? Recognizing and understanding this paradox of doubt is the key to becoming a person of vision. Doubt can be either positive or negative. It can be our greatest asset or our worst liability. It can mold us into winners or destine us to be losers. The difference is a difference in kind . . . are you an honest or skeptical doubter? All of us doubt. There is no escaping that. The question is not do you ever doubt, but what kind of a doubter are you?

HONEST VERSUS SKEPTICAL DOUBT

You might expect that a book of faith like the Bible would condemn doubt, especially doubting God. In fact, the Bible doesn't condemn doubt; it recognizes it honestly and esteems its benefits. Some of the greatest people of the Bible struggled with severe doubts. One Bible prophet named Habakkuk went as far as to build a doubting tower from whence he refused to move until his doubts disappeared. The most famous doubter of all, Doubting Thomas, stubbornly refused to believe the accounts of his friends about the resurrection of Jesus until he saw Him personally. He did see Jesus, and he did believe. The pages of the Bible are filled with men and women who doubted all types of truth. To doubt is not a failure. It is what you do with those doubts that determines whether doubt will win over you or you will win over doubt.

If we can, let's go back to our story of Doubting Thomas in John 20. All eleven of Jesus's remaining disciples had just witnessed His death. They were hiding away from the local authorities, fearing the same fate might be waiting for them. A couple of days later they were shocked with the report that Jesus' body was missing. Some even insisted that they had seen Him alive! While they argued over whether this might be true, they all became convinced when Jesus showed up in the house with them. All were convinced except one—Thomas. Thomas must have been out getting supplies when all this excitement was taking place. He returned to find his buddies buzzing with excitement. In the famous dialogue that followed, Thomas said he would not believe until he was able to touch the scarred hands and the pierced side of the Jesus he had seen die just days earlier. It was one week later when Thomas had his wish granted. Jesus came again to the same house, and this time Thomas was there. He believed just as the others had.

This all sounds like just another Bible story until we ask the question, "Why was Thomas even in that house one week later?" Think about it. These ten buddies of Thomas have just witnessed what they believe is a history-changing event in the resurrection of

Jesus. What do you think they were talking about for the week after Jesus's first appearance to them? How could they have talked about anything but the Jesus who they saw die and who was now very much alive! What did Thomas have to say, since he didn't even believe that yet? We see in Thomas an example of an honest doubter. He had legitimate and serious doubts, and yet he hung around for a week in what had to be an uncomfortable environment as the only nonbeliever in the group. Thomas had doubts, but he sincerely wanted to discover the truth. Because he waited and searched for answers, he found them. Honest doubters don't make important decisions based on emotions or past failures, but based on the facts. The secret is that honest doubters withhold judgment until they have all the facts.

Skeptical doubters, on the other hand, approach doubt from an entirely different perspective. A skeptical doubter in Thomas's place would have taken the opportunity to leave that bunch of resurrection fanatics and gone back to the regular career he had left three years earlier. Skeptical doubters use their doubt as an excuse not to do what they didn't want to do anyway. Before getting the facts, a young man declines a business opportunity because of his preconceived ideas about the business. The hidden reason? He doesn't really want to risk personal failure. A middle-aged woman doesn't develop her faith because of a bad experience in a church as a child. The hidden reason? She won't deal with her inner anger toward God. The skeptical doubter often becomes discouraged, disillusioned, and even cynical and unhappy. In these situations and many others like them, honest doubt would solve the problem by dealing with the root issues and moving on.

We all have doubts in nearly every area of our lives. Successful people develop a mindset of honest doubt. They embrace doubt as an ally to help them discover truth. They believe that, with God's help, they can accomplish great things in life. For you, doubt can be your best friend or your worst enemy. As with Aristotle, doubt can lead you to truth, or doubt can lead you to pessimism and discouragement. The choice is yours.

PRINCIPLE #2

You can get a clear picture of the difference your life can make.

We have talked several times about the Apostle Paul. A national magazine did a cover story recently on Paul, correctly crediting him with a great deal of the spread of early Christianity. He was a marvelously deep and interesting man. The depth of his skills, gifts, and determination is legendary. Through his writings we gain insight into his psyche. Paul had many intense emotions; many remind us of ourselves. As gifted as he was, he often saw himself as a highly unlikely candidate for success. At one point he even claimed that God must have saved him to prove a point . . . that He could save anybody! Paul may have been a rough character before he found faith in God, but there certainly were rougher ones. We think there is an interesting nugget of truth to be found there.

FACT #2

Often people with the greatest potential are the least able to see that potential.

Many of us can identify with that. We have often heard it said that the reason we don't accomplish more in life is that we don't expect more than enough of ourselves. We agree with that statement. We agree with this statement more: We don't accomplish more in life because we don't expect more of God. The greatest discovery in life is finding God's vision and purpose for your life. There is something wonderful that happens when you discover direction in life. Kevin McCarthy, in his book *The On-Purpose Person*, tells a charming story of a conversation between "the man" and Perry.

> *"What do you think is our greatest challenge and*
> *our greatest fear?" asked Perry.*
> *The man thought for a moment, then said, "I guess*
> *knowing that we have purpose. That we're not*
> *simply a freak of nature or a random occurrence*
> *in outer space. I want to know that my life has*
> *significance."*
> *"I think you're right about that," Perry agreed.*
> *"Aren't we first and foremost spiritual beings*
> *wanting to know that there's a reason why we're*
> *here?"*
> *"Absolutely, Perry. It just doesn't make sense*
> *sometimes. Yet I'm here. That's reason enough,*
> *cause if I wasn't supposed to be here, I guess I*
> *wouldn't be."*
> *"State it positively. Your life has meaning, no matter*
> *what your condition or situation. You have a*
> *special purpose that's as individual as your*
> *fingerprints, and it isn't too late to act on it."*[6]

We have never known anyone who didn't feel, deep down, a sense of significance. A sense that their life mattered and they could do something that would make a difference. Maybe that feeling has been stuffed and stifled for many years, but all of us have it. Life sometimes batters you down until you are willing to accept that an ordinary person like you with an ordinary life like yours will only be able to do ordinary things. It was never intended to be that way. Our firm belief is that God uses ordinary people for extraordinary purposes. He is looking for men and women who are willing to believe that. That is the beginning of vision. Discovering God's dream for you. You may be thinking that this sounds very much like our discussion concerning self-confidence and self-esteem. Vision moves far beyond self-esteem. Self-esteem is coming to the place where you believe that you are unique and have something significant to offer the world. Vision goes to the next level. Vision creates a captivating picture of that internal belief that is specific, identifiable, and helps to make it a reality.

PRINCIPLE #3

Your gifts and abilities increase as you use them!

What would you like to do better? If you could reach your dream, what would it be? Many fail to dream big because they are so keenly aware of their own faults. This is a mistake, because your faults do not keep you from reaching your dream. Every accomplished person we have ever known had glaring faults of some kind. One of the reasons biographies are so popular is that they show how human our heroes really are. All of us have strengths. All of us have weaknesses. The amount of talent or ability you have is not nearly as important as what you do with that talent and ability.

FACT #3

Less talented people often accomplish feats beyond their abilities.

We have already seen many examples of this. How does this happen? Simple. Your abilities increase as you use them. Negatively, the same truth applies. We often say to people with whom we work, "Use it or lose it." When you allow your gifts to lie stagnant and under-used, they become rusty, and you will eventually lose them.

Craig's father-in-law Ben lived an amazing life as a child. He was born in China after his parents fled across the mountains to escape communist Russia. He was seventeen years old before his family moved to America. He learned English, graduated from high school and college, married an American girl, and is now a respected pastor of an English-speaking church. For his first seventeen years the only language he knew and spoke was Russian. But after speaking primarily English for over thirty years, Ben found that he often struggled to speak in extended conversations in Russian. His sporadic use of his native tongue resulted in the diminished ability of a skill that was once second nature to him. You will find that true in all of life. Any skill that you do not use you will lose. On the contrary, when you begin fully using the abilities you already possess, you will find that your talents will grow accordingly.

All of us are sometimes guilty of wanting to build our house before we have laid the foundation. But you can't expect responsibility, influence, money, power, or respect until you have built the character traits of being responsible, having integrity, and earning respect. Likewise you can't bemoan your lack of skills when you are not using the skill you possess now. You may be thinking that this sounds like great rhetoric, but you're not convinced. C. S. Lewis was a famous skeptic of the Christian faith who writes how he was surprised by joy. Unexpectedly and unwillingly, he discovered faith in God.[7] The joy that he found was more than he could have hoped for. We are convinced that if you use principles of vision as we have discussed them, you may find yourself surprised by joy. You will likely discover that you have more talents than you thought, more skills than you knew, and more dreams than you imagined. And, when you get started, it only grows and grows.

If you can, begin painting a picture of what you want your life to look like. God has wonderful things in store for those who will accept them. Vision is for you. Are you willing to honestly deal with your doubts, believe that you can make a difference, and begin today with what you have to work? It is an exciting journey if you are up to it.

11

DISCOVERING THE POWER OF PERSONAL VISION

*"I find the great thing in this world is not so much where we stand,
as in what direction we are moving: To reach the port of
heaven, we must sail sometimes with the wind and sometimes
against it – but we must sail, and not drift, nor lie at anchor."*[1]
OLIVER WENDELL HOLMES

WHEN HELEN KELLER WAS
once asked if there were anything worse than being blind, she
answered, "Yes! Being able to see and having no vision." We like
the way Tony Campolo puts it in his book on success: "The Bible
makes a big deal about visions. It tells us that without them we are
all dead" (PROVERBS 29:18).[2] "Okay," you say, "I'm starting to get
convinced. How do I really get a handle on finding my vision?"
The first step is to be certain that you understand vision. Simply
put, your vision is your perfect ideal for life. While we'll talk about

that more in a moment, you can be sure of one thing. Nothing will happen in your life until you know and are able to communicate your vision for each area of your life. You shape your vision, and then your vision shapes you. Without a vision you are not living; you are existing.

WHAT IS VISION?

Vision is really not all that complicated. Vision is your perfect ideal for your life, including your career, your family, your personal life, and your relationship with God. Vision is a picture of the future you would like to have. Once you have developed your vision related to each of those areas, the vision helps keep you on track. Vision keeps you pressing on, and vision also helps keep your life in balance. However, it isn't quite as simple as it sounds. Vision is really the development of a new mindset. Here are some ideas that will help clarify your understanding of vision.

VISION IS SEEING REALITY IN ADVANCE

Most great accomplishments throughout history have been built by people with vision. The typical person without vision becomes altogether stuck in the way things are in the present. A person with vision is able to see the future the way it will be, not simply the way it is now. The person without vision grieves over how things are. The person of vision works to change the way things are.

Before 1891, horses and carriages filled hard dirt streets, and American cities were pothole-laden, dusty, sometimes muddy places to live and work. George Bartholomew had a dream for a better future. In the back room of his family pharmacy, located in his hometown of Bellefontaine, Ohio, he was experimenting with a concoction of limestone, clay, and marl glued together with a gray powder that he had refined and called "cement." He believed that streets of his "artificial stone" would revolutionize the transportation system of the young United States.

Few had any idea of the revolutionary implications of this new discovery. In fact, the citizens and city officials of Bellefontaine were so skeptical and doubtful that they put up quite a roadblock to this world-changing and innovative way to build streets, sidewalks, and front porches. They were not at all convinced that Bartholomew's idea would work. It took two full years to merely convince the city to let him try his project within the city. Even after they agreed to let him test his new breakthrough, there were harsh stipulations. Bartholomew had to donate the materials and labor for a 100' x 8' test section on Main Street. He also had to post a five thousand dollar performance bond (in 1891 money!) guaranteeing that the pavement would last five years.

Undoubtedly many of the scoffers were embarrassed by the results. The project was a great success. By 1894, the remainder of Main Street was paved, and parts of the concrete pavement was still in service during the 1960s, nearly seventy years after being laid. Bellefontaine became the little town that sparked a revolution, ushering in the age of the automobile, mass industry, and the United States production and delivery system. Today a monument in Bellefontaine reads, "Here started the better roads movement which has given our citizens from coast to coast swift and sure transportation." We would add, "because of the vision of one man, George Bartholomew."[3]

Many great visionaries have suffered similar obstacles in trying to convince the masses what the future could be like. History is filled with people noted not for their vision but for their lack of ability to see what the future would hold. In 1926, Lee de Forest, the inventor of the cathode ray tube said, "While theoretically television may be feasible, commercially and financially I consider it an impossibility, a development of which we need waste little time dreaming."[4] In 1943, Thomas J. Watson, chairman of the board for IBM, said, "I think there is a world market for about five computers."[5] The recording company executive who turned down the Beatles in 1962 said, "We don't think they will do anything in this market. Guitar groups are on the way out."[6] In the magazine *Business Week* in 1968 it was written, "With over 15 types of foreign cars already on sale here, the Japanese auto industry isn't likely to carve out a big share of the market for itself."[7] It's easy for us to laugh, but we shouldn't be too hard on these people because they represented the view of the majority. Few are able to capture the power of vision. These are, in retrospect, humorous examples and positive reminders to stretch your ability to see the future in advance. For you the real question is, "What am I failing to see that my future could be?"

VISION VERSUS FANTASY

What do you see for your future in the various areas of your life? To set yourself free to dream about your future can be a fun project. But you are ahead of the game if you are wondering what the difference is between fantasizing about having a million-dollar-a-day job and having a real vision for your career. After all, anyone can dream about what he would like in life. Walter Mitty was a master daydreamer. You may have read James Thurber's amusing short story where his timid, browbeaten character named Walter Mitty fantasized about being everything from a world-famous surgeon to a champion race car driver, all in the same trip to the doctor. In reality he was little more than an intimidated husband who escaped reality through his incessant daydreaming.[8]

Vision is far and away different from fantasy. The difference has nothing to do with size. You can't have too big of a vision. The difference: Vision is convinced something will happen. Fantasy hopes something will happen. Vision is firmly rooted in the ability to see the future reality of something that hasn't yet happened. Fantasy would be happy if something happened in the future. Vision is set to work towards its goal. Fantasy simply wants it to happen without having to work for it. To be more specific, vision is a clear mental picture of a preferable future. Go ahead. Get a vision that's as big as you can believe. We have found that a major challenge related to vision is not that people dream too big, but that they dream too small. Certainly reality checks are important. "Can I see this happening? Am I willing to work to make this happen?" But dream big. The only limit to the size of your vision is how much you can honestly believe. We will say it again. The reason you don't accomplish more is that you don't plan for more through building your vision!

VISION IS SEEING SOLUTIONS TO PROBLEMS

A positive outlook on life is immensely important. If you haven't yet discovered it, life is a series of challenges and difficulties, one after the other. We don't think that this is pessimistic; it's just fact. Recognizing, then, that this is his lot in life, the person of vision takes this as his motto: "Optimism is not denying the presence of difficulty but recognizing that there is no difficulty too big for God to help me solve." Vision is the ability to see solutions to problems.

Visionary people are solution-oriented, and not problem-oriented. We all encounter problems regularly. The most natural way to deal with difficulty is to worry. Often when faced with difficult challenges, you may focus on the problem itself. As you focus on the problem, it gets bigger and bigger until you finally conclude that it is too big to handle. This is what ordinary, visionless people do, but it is not the mode of operation for the person of vision. The visionary trains himself to look at every challenge in life with an attitude that says, "There is a solution to this. I will find it." What we are describing is a habit of thinking. You shouldn't think, "Now, I'm stuck." You should think, "How am I going to get out?" You shouldn't say, "Now, what do I do?" You should say, "What are my options?" Vision is an attitude which turns to solutions instead of wallowing in the obvious.

We can only hope that no one will be reading our mail a hundred years from now, but Martin Van Buren, then Governor of New York and later President, has left us another infamous example of a lack of vision.

To President Jackson:

The canal system of this country is being threatened by the spread of a new form of transportation known as "railroads." The Federal Government must preserve the canals for the following reasons:

One. If canal boats are supplanted by "railroads," serious unemployment will result. Captains, cooks, drivers, hostlers, repairmen and lock tenders will be left without means of livelihood, not to mention the numerous farmers now employed in growing hay for the horses.

Two. Boat builders would suffer, and towline, whip and harness makers would be left destitute.

Three. Canal boats are absolutely essential to the defense of the United States. In the event of the expected trouble with England, the Erie Canal would be the only means by which we could ever move the supplies so vital to waging a modern war.

As you know, Mr. President, "railroad" carriages are pulled at the enormous speed of fifteen miles per hour by engines which, in addition to endangering life and limb of passengers, roar and snort their way through the countryside, setting fires to crops, scattering the livestock and frightening women and children. The almighty certainly never intended that people should travel at such breakneck speed.

MARTIN VAN BUREN
GOVERNOR OF NEW YORK[9]

This is a prime example of someone having no vision, searching for all the problems rather than looking for the solution or for the potential of doing things a new way.

History has answered the short-sighted objections of Van Buren, and his protest sheds light on another important aspect of vision. People of vision must be willing and able to let go of the fear of change. It is a part of the human condition to fight change. Most of us not only like, but need security. Vision means embracing change. It means stepping out where things are uncomfortable for you. It means challenging your preconceived ideas and your ingrained habits of lifestyle and thinking. New challenges require new solutions, and those who get left behind are those who refuse to change with the times. In our day, no one can afford to be stuck in the past. Our fast-paced society of technological revolutions demands that you be willing and able to see new things in new ways. What new solutions can you bring to your job, your family, or your challenges with your faith? The person of vision is not only ready for change, he is usually leading the way in initiating it.

Practical Ideas for Being Solution-Centered

STEP #1

When encountering a challenge, develop the habit of saying to yourself, "This difficulty is not too big for me and God to handle." You can sometimes come to the end of your abilities. But if you have been teaming up with God, no problem is too large for God to handle. Is that something you really believe? It is a life-transforming truth. Forming a habit of continuously reminding yourself of that truth is the beginning of becoming a solution-centered person. Soon this will become such an ingrained practice that you no longer have to think about it. Until then, keep thinking about it. "God is bigger than my problem."

STEP #2

Get advice from other solution-oriented people. Call on those relationships you have been cultivating. There is power when like-minded people put their minds together. There is amazing diversity in the way different people, with different outlooks and backgrounds, view situations. Take advantage of that great resource.

STEP #3

List four or five potential solutions to the situation you are facing.

Our minds have the ability to find dormant ideas that we didn't know existed inside of us. Brainstorming is a powerful way of finding solutions to problems. When you stretch yourself you may be surprised at what you discover. We make a habit of stretching our abilities so that we will be constantly improving ourselves. You will often find that there are solutions to your challenge that are waiting to be identified. The practice of extending yourself to list four or five potential solutions each time you encounter a challenge will succeed in uncovering an abundance of solutions for you. Soon this will become second nature to you as well. Until it is second nature, force yourself.

HOW DO YOU FIND YOUR VISION?

Finding your personal vision is a very personal thing. You cannot adopt another person's vision as your own. Neither can someone else get your vision for you. It is an intensely personal experience. Your vision should challenge you, inspire you, motivate you, and guide you. Your vision is your own mental picture of what you expect your life to be. It is more than worth the effort to find your personal vision. It is the only happy way to live. While we can't tell you what your vision is, we can give you some suggestions on how to find yours for yourself. Here are some thoughts.

SPEND SOME TIME ALONE

The first step in finding your personal vision is to sit down alone. The philosopher Pascal once said that most of man's problems come from an inability to sit still.[10] Amid the hustle and hectic schedule most of us keep, it is no easy task to get significant time alone to ponder the preferable future for the various areas of your life. Regular time alone in quiet meditation with God is one of the least appreciated and most powerful habits in life. Richard Foster has written extensively about the inner life, and he says that nothing significant happens until we become serious about exploring our inner self.[11] By establishing a routine time in which you are alone, you will set the stage for finding and maintaining vision. To get in touch with your vision will require time spent alone. Most of the great people of the Bible got their personal vision from God when they were alone. If it is not already a regular habit, you may find it quite challenging to set aside consistent time alone for the development and cultivation of your personal vision. Be encouraged, it will be time well spent.

ASSOCIATE WITH OTHER VISIONARIES

You have probably picked up on how important we view association with the right people. The right people here simply means others who are working to find and fulfill God's dream for them. Visionaries hang out with other visionaries. Iron sharpens iron in the same way as visionary friends sharpen one another. You will need assistance, ideas, support and encouragement to make your vision reality. A quality group of other visionaries will take you farther and more quickly than you can go it alone.

WRITE IT DOWN

A vision that is in your head can too easily leak out and be lost forever. Write your vision out for each area of your life. As you write, you will find that your thinking will become much clearer and more crystallized. Refer to your written vision often to be certain that you are making progress. Make other people whom you trust aware of your vision. That will keep you accountable and make you more apt to stay focused.

Vision is a big deal. It is the only way that you will realize your potential. Ultimately you will never discover your vision until you have included God in the process. His plan for you and His partnership with you in life are vital. Visions become meaningful when God places them in your heart. When that happens, you will see life in a completely different way. You will live life in a completely different way. You won't get stalled when you have a God-given personal vision focused on your future. Your vision can change your life and impact the world when you know it and live it.

12

FINDING THE DARING VISION YOU NEED TO SUCCEED

*"When it comes to the future, there are three kinds of people:
those who let it happen, those who make it happen,
and those who wonder what happened."*[1]
JOHN M. RICHARDSON, JR.

ADARING VISION BEGAN IN Portland, Oregon, in the early 1960s. Philip Knight decided to sell imported running shoes out of the back of his station wagon. His college coach, William Bowerman, joined him in 1963, and they modified their imported shoes to improve their quality. Their start-up investment for their little shoe company was all of one thousand dollars. Thirty years after those unpretentious beginnings, Nike Incorporated has a market value of $3.1 billion. Nike not only markets the phrase but was born out of the concept, "Just Do It!"[2]

In 1959, two young visionaries were living by the same motto long before it was a marketing slogan. Jay Van Andel and Richard DeVos were dreamers who wanted to work for themselves. In their basements they began a small shoestring business selling household supplies. They called their business the Amway Corporation, and its growth from modest origins to a seven billion dollar corporation has become legendary in entrepreneurial circles. These are two small examples of how modest beginnings could produce such world-changing results. How does it happen? Vision!

The essence of vision lies in the fact that it is not ordinary. Vision is an extraordinary quality that has a way of benefiting everyone. Vision brings out the best in us personally; vision elicits cooperation from others, drawing like-minded people like a magnet; and vision has been behind the bulk of history's great discoveries and accomplishments. Vision is a unique and uncommon quality in people. With that being the case, obtaining it will require a certain sense of boldness and fearlessness. There is very little success in life that doesn't involve some risk. How will you find the faith to capture a daring vision for life? We hope to give you some support in doing that with the help of this phenomenal story.

DARING VISION DOESN'T NEED ALL THE ANSWERS

We have found that this story of the Apostle Peter, found in Matthew 14, is an excellent example of daring vision. Jesus had just performed a fantastic miracle among some ten thousand or more people. The scene where the miracle had taken place was beginning to get out of hand. More than becoming a fiasco, it was getting dangerous, and Jesus recognized it. Taking control, Jesus told His twelve disciples to get into a boat and head across the Sea of Galilee while He dispersed the crowd. They did as Jesus asked, and several hours later found themselves in an extremely precarious predicament. As often happens on the Sea of Galilee, a sudden but powerful storm had risen, and all twelve of the disciples were in a life-threatening situation. Many of these men were fishermen and knew the peril of being on this sea in the center of a Middle Eastern storm. It was three o'clock in the morning, and all of them were wet, cold, tired, and scared. The wind was howling, the waves were crashing against the boat, and the rain was pelting them.

Suddenly, in the midst of this chaotic situation, someone, perhaps Philip, saw the moonlit figure of a person walking on the water. They all rubbed their eyes in disbelief and didn't know what to think of the situation. How could this be real? Then out of the darkness they heard a familiar voice. It was Jesus saying, "Don't be afraid. It is I." As you can imagine, they were all in a state of shock and probably rather speechless at this point. Then Peter broke the silence with a stunning request. "Jesus, if that's You, let me come out there with You." Wow! What a thought. As unexpected as the question was, the equally surprising response from Jesus was, "Come on!" And then to top off this whole extraordinary experience, the Bible tells us that Peter got down out of the boat and walked on the water to go to Jesus.

What's the point of this amazing story? The point is that Peter shows us a model of daring faith. Anyone who knows Peter at all knows that his request to go to Jesus was anything but well thought out. Peter was impetuous and thoroughly unpredictable.

There were no risk analyses with him. No proverbial weighing of the advantages and disadvantages of such a request to walk on the water. A simple blurt off the tip of the tongue was doubtless all it was. Yet, having made the request, Peter was more than ready to follow through after Jesus told him to come join Him.

The lessons here are simple but powerful. Clearly, for Peter, daring faith didn't need all the answers. In fact, daring vision can't have all the answers. That is exactly why it is visionary. Peter didn't have to know the details of how he could walk on water; he didn't ask for the physics equations that would show this to be feasible. He just did it. You will never develop a captivating and life-changing vision as long as you try to answer every detail. Philip Knight and William Bowerman didn't know all the answers as to how Nike would be transformed into a sports apparel powerhouse. It was vision. Steven Jobs and Steven Wosniac, founders of Apple Computer, didn't have all the answers on how to make their computers user-friendly giants in the ultra-competitive computer market. They had a vision and found the answers as they went along. Jack Kennedy didn't wait for technological questions to be answered before he announced that we would put a man on the moon. He just communicated his vision and believed there was a way to make it possible. There was, and we did. We could say the same for Leonardo da Vinci, Henry Ford, Amelia Earhart, Benjamin Franklin, Thomas Edison, and Susan B. Anthony, as well for as a host of other great visionaries.

But more significant than all of that, we could say the same for the John Does, the Jane Smiths, the Peter Joneses, and Mary Millers throughout the world who have simply allowed their vision to help them create a better life for themselves and for their families. While great leaders and visionaries are inspiring for us, they are not always ones to which we can relate. We could personally tell of people we know whose vision for a better future made a good family better, a good job a great career, a rocky financial situation a personal strength. Vision is not only for the rich and famous, for presidents, diplomats, inventors and geniuses. Vision literally is for all people. Vision is for you.

The wise man Solomon once said, "If you wait for perfect conditions, you'll never get anything done" (ECCLESIASTES 11:4 LB). Ask yourself this question: "What am I waiting to do because I don't understand?" The answer to that question may tell you what is keeping you from an extraordinary vision in life. Certainly we don't want to espouse ignorant vision that is not rooted in reality and that is unattainable. But it is possible to overthink things and to be overly critical. There is a huge difference between reasonable faith and having all the answers. Vision is reasonable, but there will always be questions that are unanswerable. What is your perfect ideal for your life? What is keeping you from reaching out to obtain it starting today?

DARING FAITH ALWAYS DEMANDS INITIATING ACTION

Well, we've left Peter suspended on the edge of that boat. As we pick up where we left off, we discover that Peter succeeded. He actually walked on the water. We don't know of anyone before or since who has done it, but Peter walked on water. As hard as it is to comprehend, we can only conclude that Peter had enough faith to do that impossible feat. But buried in this astonishing story there is something extremely profound. Peter never would have walked on the water until he got out of the boat. All of his faith would have been useless until he took the fateful step over the edge. The world is filled with people who have dormant and undeveloped visions that need to be let loose. Their vision for life is never cultivated, never fleshed out, and never fulfilled. They have the capacity for vision, but it is simply wasting away inside them.

We all have our own boats. Just like those twelve disciples, you feel much safer in your boat than you do getting out where you have never been. Your boat is that place where you feel comfortable and secure. It is that which you understand and can see. Venturing beyond those secure surroundings is a threatening proposition. To be a person of vision frequently means teetering on the edge of where things are uncomfortable and where you are at great risk to fail. You will constantly be stretched beyond your present abilities. Such is the life of the visionary. Though it may seem uncomfortable, it is the only road that allows you to accomplish in life what is otherwise impossible, like . . . inventing cement, building a computer powerhouse, or walking on water. It is the only way to realize the potential with which God has blessed you. There are uncharted waters out there and discoveries galore which are waiting for you. Don't cheat the world of your gift of vision. What action do you know you need to take right now to make your vision a reality? It begins with the first step.

DARING FAITH WILL SOMETIMES LEAD YOU TO CRASH

Up to this point our story with Peter has been one of daring, faith, and success. But events soon began to take a different direction.

Peter began to sink. It didn't happen without good reason. We can understand fully what happened to Peter. Peter was smiling and enthusiastic as he walked on the water in the direction of Jesus. Suddenly and without warning, his peripheral vision picked up a gigantic wave that appeared to be coming right towards him. He turned. He saw not just one wave, but a sea of terrifying and deadly waves. He forgot about Jesus. He forgot about walking on the water. He was dumbstruck by the mass of waves which surrounded him, and he began to sink.

Peter's experience is not unlike that of many of us. Daring vision will sometimes lead you to crash. But are you more worried about failure than you should be? Failure is highly overrated. Science is filled with illustrations of great discoveries that were stumbled onto by blind luck, or maybe even the result of mistakes. An example of this is Velcro. The discovery of Velcro has changed the way we live. Velcro is no longer a novelty, but a highly developed and necessary fastener for all kinds of complicated applications. Velcro was discovered in the early 1950s, not by some scientist in his lab, but by an irritated Swiss hiker who was picking cockleburs off his jacket when he began wondering what made them stick so tenaciously. He discovered under a microscope that tiny hooks covering the cockleburs became caught in the fabric of clothing.[2] The rest is history. The discovery of penicillin, X-rays, and Teflon were all similar types of accidental breakthroughs.

Vision and crashing will go hand in hand. There is no way to avoid it. Maybe you can't recover from a bad experience of a failed attempt in the past. Or perhaps you falter each time you take a new visionary step because you begin to focus on your present problems, questions, or limitations. Or it may be that you are paralyzed by fear of the future and that which is unknown and uncertain. The pressures of life will squeeze the life and the vision out of you if you let them. Don't give in that easily. When you focus on your vision, the pressures and problems of life will begin to look smaller and smaller and smaller. When it comes to vision, you can't afford to be shy.

DARING FAITH IS ALWAYS WORTH THE RISK

All of this talk about risk is very unsettling for some. And then there are those personalities who find that risk is a reward in and of itself. A high-octane lifestyle for them is not just acceptable, it's invited and even necessary. On the other hand, you may be one of many who enjoy a much safer existence and find the whole concept of risk unsettling and stressful. We want you to be encouraged to know that daring vision is always worth the risk. To live life without daring vision is like jumping into a ship with the dream of discovering a new continent while never leaving the harbor. You batten down your supplies, study your navigational charts, christen the voyage, but refuse to untie the rope from the dock. You can't be happy living life like that. Untie the rope. Put up your sails and venture into the high seas. There is mystery, danger, adventure, and fulfillment out there. You will never realize your potential while you putt around at the dock. You will only discover who God created you to be when you set out to the open sea. Daring faith is always, always, always worth the risk. Even if you crash you can always rest in the knowledge that you went down in the quest for your dream.

To walk down the ancient streets of Rome is to get an

education in the school of art and history. Author and Catholic priest Henri Nouwen describes one of his strolls down a Roman street when he was reminded of this story. A little boy watched one day as a sculptor had a enormous piece of marble unloaded and placed inside his studio. With great curiosity the boy watched as the sculptor chiseled and pried on the marble chunk. Large and small pieces of marble fell everywhere. He had no idea what was happening, and soon he became bored and left to find something more interesting to do. A few weeks passed, and the boy visited again at the studio of his sculptor friend. When he walked into the room, he stood with his mouth agape at the sight of the large, powerful lion sitting in the place where the marble block had stood before. With great excitement the boy ran to the sculptor and asked, "How did you know there was a lion in that marble?"[3]

Where everyone else saw a block of marble, this sculptor saw a hungry lion. Michelangelo saw a loving mother carrying her dead son on her lap; in another block, he saw a young David ready to hurl a stone at the mammoth Goliath. "Thus," Nouwen says, "the skillful artist is a liberator who frees from their bondage the figures that have been hidden for billions of years inside the marble, unable to reveal their true identity." What wonderful and fulfilling life is trapped inside of you, waiting to have its identity unleashed and set free by the power of personal vision? What risk is too great when it comes to discovering the triumph of a life lived to its fullest? We know that you won't be disappointed when you embark on a journey like that one. Daring faith may not have all the answers. It always requires taking action. It may include a few crash landings. But it is always worth the risk.

CONCLUSION

"We are free up to the point of choice,
then the choice controls the chooser."[1]
MARY CROWLEY

WE HEARD ABOUT A NAVAL
training session taking place in the Bay recently. The weather was
perilous with thick fog, drenching rains, and unwieldy winds. Late
into the first day of maneuvers a navy battleship saw a light
straight ahead and knew that a collision would be imminent. The
commander grabbed the radio and made this transmission: "We
are on a collision course, you must change your direction." In a
moment came the response: "You are correct. We are on a collision
course, but you must change your direction." To this the commander

responded with increasing urgency: "This is a naval commander! You must change direction!" Again the response: "I am a simple seaman. Nonetheless, you must change your direction." Losing patience the commander retorted angrily, "This is a navy battleship. You must change direction!" "I am sorry, sir," came the reply, "This is a lighthouse and you must change direction."

Sometimes the most difficult thing to do in life is to change course. Old habits, present comfort zones, and new attitudes all resist the sweeping impact that change will bring to our lives.

Stubbornness leads us to resist it. Fear keeps us from attempting it. Difficulty keeps us from succeeding at it. Change seldom comes easily.

This book you've just read is all about change. The interesting thing about change is that no one can do it for you. It is an entirely independent discipline. Sergei Beloglazov is widely known as possibly the greatest Olympic wrestler of all time. Only the Soviet boycott of the 1984 Los Angeles Olympics kept Sergei from winning three straight Olympic gold medals. Sergei was virtually unbeatable. When asked the secret of his incredible success, he responded in enthusiastic but broken English, "Every move I practiced thousands of times . . . thousands of times!" This must be what Solomon meant when he said:

> *If the ax is dull and its edge unsharpened, more strength*
> *is needed but skill will bring success.*
>
> ECCLESIASTES 10:10

If you long to really throw away your crutches and realize your potential, maintaining your focus on those areas requiring change is a necessity. Reading has been the easy part. Change is now your great challenge.

Let us preface this illustration by saying that we are by no means mechanics. We know exactly how to get to our local repair shop, but we only have a vague idea of how our engine works. With that understood, suffer with us through this analogy. We know that a tuned engine runs with the most efficiency. If an engine is untuned, the engine cannot run at peak performance. It will use excessive amounts of fuel, lack needed power, and potentially leave you stranded somewhere along the side of the road. Most car owners know that regular and routine maintenance extends engine life and saves money in the long run.

Never underestimate the power of a tuned-up, efficiently running life. When we make necessary changes and our life is running at peak performance, we will notice numerous benefits.

REDUCED FRUSTRATION

A Russian immigrant was having great difficulty with the English language. His teacher tried to help him out by teaching him a simple way to order at a restaurant. He said, "In any American restaurant you simply say, 'Hamburger, fries, coke.' Can you say that?" The Russian man repeated the phrase, "Hamburger, fries, coke." Off he went, and for an entire week his diet consisted of hamburgers, fries and coke. The next week he told his teacher that he was very tired of eating the same thing and wanted to order a new meal. "Okay." The teacher said, "Next time you go to breakfast say, "Egg, toast, juice.'" The next morning the Russian man went to breakfast. His waitress came to take his order to which he responded, "Egg, toast, juice." "All right," said the waitress, "would you like your eggs scrambled, fried, poached or hard boiled? Would like your toast to be white, wheat, rye, or sourdough? For juice we have orange, grapefruit, apple, or grape. Which would you like?" The Russian man thought for a moment and replied, "Hamburger, fries, coke!"

We have found that people today are generally less patient and more uptight. Frustration is high as people find their lives going in every direction, unable to find the right focus. Such frustrations can be erased when we are running with a well-tuned life.

INCREASED INCENTIVE

A small taste of honey only whets our appetite for more. Once we begin to see the benefits which come from the right kind of change, we will be motivated to continue. There is no greater incentive than positive results. As the old adage goes, "Nothing succeeds like success."

What would give you incentive to pick your way, piece by piece, through a reeking landfill? We read an article recently which began, "Dale Miller's laundry may have cost him a life on Easy Street." Apparently, Dale had picked the right numbers in Florida's $20 million jackpot. The only problem was that he had inadvertently washed his winning ticket in the pocket of his shirt in Sunday morning's laundry. Retrieving the shirt, he found that the ticket was only a ball and he threw it away. But on Monday, he discovered that the Florida Lottery Commission could perform tests to authenticate a mutilated ticket if he could present it to them. By then, Miller's trash had already been picked up by a garbage truck. He hurried out to the Tomoka landfill and arrived in time to meet the truck carrying his trash. He and a friend braved the stench to pick through the truck's load. It was to no avail. The lottery ticket was gone!

Hundreds of people have discovered firsthand that the lottery is no answer to prayer. Often the winnings do more harm than good. People unprepared for wealth are seldom savvy enough to handle its power. We're not promising life on Easy Street, but we will say without reservation that the greatest incentive you will find to change your life is the beneficial effect that positive change will have on you. It is worth the dig. The joy these positive changes will bring will make a $20 million dollar jackpot pale in comparison. That's no overstatement. There is a great reward awaiting you. Let's throw away the crutches. Let's sail!

ENDNOTES

FOREWORD
1. Peggy Anderson, *Great Quotes from Great Leaders* (Lombard, IL: Successories Publishing, 1990), p. 103.

INTRODUCTION
1. Anderson, *Great Quotes from Great Leaders,* p. 7.

———————————————— PART ONE ————————————————

1. Anderson, *Great Quotes from Great Leaders,* p. 113

CHAPTER ONE
2. Anderson, *Great Quotes from Great Leaders,* p. 61.

CHAPTER TWO
1. Anderson, *Great Quotes from Great Leaders,* p. 12.

CHAPTER THREE
1. Kevin W. McCarthy, *The On-Purpose Person* (Colorado Springs: Pinon Press, 1992), p. 129.
2. Author, "Title of Article," *U.S. News & World Report* (Aug. 6, 1990), pg. 62; Author, "Title of Article," *Prevention* (June 1991), pg. 33.

———————————————— PART TWO ————————————————

1. Anderson, *Great Quotes from Great Leaders,* p. 41.

CHAPTER FOUR
2. *New Webster's Dictionary of Quotations and Famous Phrases,* (New York: Berkley Books, 1987), p. 193.
3. Author, "Title of Article," *Psychology Today* (October 1983), pp. 80-81.
4. Author, "Title of Article," *U.S. News & World Report* (October 1983).
5. *New Webster's Dictionary of Quotations and Famous Phrases,* p. 205.

CHAPTER FIVE
1. Anderson, *Great Quotes from Great Leaders,* p. 25.
2. Joe Griffith, *Speakers Library of Business Stories, Anecdotes, and Humor* (Englewood Cliffs, NJ: Prentice-Hall, 1990), p. 298-99.
3. Ibid.
4. Ibid.

CHAPTER SIX
1. William Safire and Leonard Safir, *Words of Wisdom* (New York: Simon and Schuster, 1989), p. 101.

──────────── PART THREE ────────────

1. Anderson, *Great Quotes from Great Leaders,* p. 77.
2. Critical and Miscellaneous Essays (Richter, 1827), found in: *Bartlett's Familiar Quotations* by John Bartlett, 15th ed. (1st ed. 1855) (Boston: Little, Brown and Company, 1980), p. 474.
3. Laurence J. Peter, *Peter's Quotations* (New York: Bantam Books, 1977), p. 77.

CHAPTER SEVEN
4. Jack Canfield and Mark Victor Hansen, *A Second Helping of Chicken Soup for the Soul* (Deerfield Beach, FL: Health Communications, Inc., 1995), p. 185.
5. Words by William J. and Gloria Gaither. Music by William J. Gaither. Copyright ©1975 by William J. Gaither.

CHAPTER EIGHT
1. Canfield and Hansen, *A Second Helping of Chicken Soup for the Soul,* p. 230.
2. John R. Claypool, *The Preaching Event* (Waco, TX: Word Books, 1980), p. 30.
3. *The Amplified New Testament* (Grand Rapids, MI: Zondervan, 1958).
4. Griffith, *Speakers Library of Business Stories, Anecdotes, and Humor,* p. 102.

CHAPTER NINE
1. Canfield and Hansen, *A Second Helping of Chicken Soup for the Soul,* p. 288.
2. Griffith, *Speakers Library of Business Stories, Anecdotes, and Humor,* p. 112.
3. Ibid.
4. Canfield and Hansen, *A Second Helping of Chicken Soup for the Soul,* p. 252-53.
5. Griffith, *Speakers Library of Business Stories, Anecdotes, and Humor,* p. 248.
6. Ibid.
7. Dave and Jan Dravecky, *When You Can't Come Back* (Grand Rapids, MI: Zondervan; San Francisco: Harper San Francisco, 1992), p. 21.
8. Ibid., p. 18.

──────────── PART FOUR ────────────

1. Anderson, *Great Quotes from Great Leaders,* p. 105.

CHAPTER TEN
2. Zig Ziglar, *Top Performance* (Old Tappan, NJ: Fleming H. Revell Co., 1986), p. 140.
3. Peter, *Peter's Quotations,* p. 156.
4. Ibid.
5. Ibid., p. 155.
6. McCarthy, *The On-Purpose Person,* p. 180.
7. C.S. Lewis, *Surprised by Joy; The Shape of My Early Life* (New York: Harcourt, Brace and Co., 1955).

CHAPTER ELEVEN

1. Burt Nanus, *Visionary Leadership* (San Francisco: Jossey-Bass Publishers, 1992), p. 133.
2. Tony Campolo, *Everything You've Heard Is Wrong* (Dallas: Word, 1992), p. 115.
3. Author, "Title of Article," *USA Today* Magazine (December 1991), p. 14.
4. Griffith, *Speakers Library of Business Stories, Anecdotes, and Humor,* p. 122.
5. Ibid.
6. Ibid.
7. Ibid.
8. James Thurber, *My World and Welcome to It* (New York: Harcourt, Brace and Co., 1937), pp. 72-81.
9. *The papers of Martin Van Buren* (on Microfilm at Stanford University [NS10290]), (Alexander, Virginia, Chadwyck: Healty 1987). February 20, 1829.
10. Peter, *Peter's Quotations,* p. 218.
11. Richard J. Foster, *Celebration of Discipline* (New York: Harper & Row,1978), pp. 1-9.

CHAPTER TWELVE

1. Foster, *Celebration of Discipline,* p. 133.
2. Royston M. Roberts, *Serendipity: Accidental Discoveries of Science* (Wiley Publishers, 1989).
3. Henri Houwen, *Clowning in Rome* (New York: Image Books, 1979), pp. 87-88.

CONCLUSION

1. Ziglar, *Top Performance,* p. 17.